**AFF
AND**

AFFORDABLE SPAS AND FITNESS RESORTS

The Insider's Guide to Health-oriented Vacations & Weekends

Ryan Vollmer

Ventana Press, Chapel Hill

Copyright © 1988 Ryan Margaret Vollmer

All rights reserved. This book may not be duplicated in any way without the expressed written consent of the publisher, except in the form of brief excerpts or quotations for the purposes of review. Making copies of this book, or any portion for any purpose other than your own, is a violation of United States copyright laws.

Published by: Ventana Press
P.O. Box 2468
Chapel Hill, NC 27515

Library of Congress Catalog Number: 87-51642
ISBN Number: 0-940087-08-1

First edition, First printing
Printed in the United States of America

Cover Design: Suzanne Anderson-Carey
Book Design: Tim Walker
Typesetting: Johnna Webb of **Pixel** Plus Desktop Publishing
Technical Editing: Lynn Jaluvka and Nancy Pipes of
　TechniProse, Inc.

The author and publisher have prepared to their best of their ability the information, prices, schedules and availability for the spas contained herein. Due to the ever-changing nature of the subject, the publisher can make no guarantee regarding validity and quality.

ACKNOWLEDGMENTS

My deepest thanks go to reporter Judith Lock for her excellent interviewing skills and tireless efforts. Her contributions played a major role in the content and completion of this book.

Additional thanks go to Lynn Ellen Echnoz for her research and reporting, and to Jim Kogel for his support and good humor.

Table of Contents

Introduction   xiii

Chapter One: **Anatomy of a Spa**   3

Chapter Two: **Northeastern Spas and Fitness Resorts**

Grand Lake Spa Hotel (CT)	11
Norwich Inn and Spa (CT)	13
Weight Watchers at The Hartford Treadway Hotel (CT)	15
Northern Pines Health Resort (ME)	17
Evernew Summer Spa Camp for Women (MA)	19
Kripalu Center (MA)	21
The Spa at Bally's (NJ)	23
Harbor Island Spa (NJ)	25
Mayfair: The Spa by the Sea (NJ)	26
The Shoreham Hotel (NJ)	28
Living Springs Retreat (NY)	30
Mohonk Mountain House (NY)	31

AFFORDABLE SPAS

New Age Health Farm (NY)	34
Omega Institute for Holistic Studies (NY)	36
Le Parker Merídien (NY)	38
Pawling Health Manor (NY)	40
Tennanah Lakeshore Lodge Spa and Retreat (NY)	42
Deerfield Manor (PA)	43
The Glass Door Spa (PA)	45
The Himalayan Institute (PA)	47
Golden Eagle Health Spa (VT)	49
New Life Spa (VT)	51
The Spa at Stowe (VT)	53

Chapter Three: **Southern Spas and Fitness Resorts**

The Fontainebleu Hilton Resort and Spa (FL)	59
Harbor Island Spa (FL)	61
Lido Spa Hotel (FL)	63
Weight Watchers at Newport Pier Holiday Inn (FL)	65
The Spa at Palm-Aire (FL)	67
Regency Health Resort and Spa (FL)	69
Russell House (FL)	70
Safety Harbor Spa and Fitness Center (FL)	72
Sonesta Sanibel Harbour Resort (FL)	74
Bluegrass Spa (KY)	76
Avenue Plaza Hotel/EuroVita Spa (LA)	78
Four Seasons Hotel and Resort (TX)	80
Guadalupe River Ranch and Health Enhancement Center (TX)	82
Lake Austin Resort Spa (TX)	84
Hartland Health Center (VA)	86
The Homestead (VA)	88
Coolfont Resort (WV)	90
The Greenbrier (WV)	92
The Woods Fitness Institute (WV)	94

Chapter Four: **Midwestern Spas and Fitness Resorts**

The Heartland (IL)	99
The Spa at French Lick Springs Golf and Tennis Resort (IN)	102
Weight Watchers at The Bartley House (MI)	104
Birdwing Spa (MN)	106
Sans Souci Health Resort (OH)	107
Akia (OK)	109
Interlaken Resort and Country Spa (WI)	111
Olympia Village Conference Center Resort Spa (WI)	113
The Wooden Door (WI)	114

Chapter Five: **Western Spas and Fitness Resorts**

Loews Ventana Canyon Resort (AZ)	119
Scottsdale Hilton Resort and Spa (AZ)	121
Tucson National Resort and Spa (AZ)	123
Weight Watchers at The Camelview Radisson Resort (AZ)	125
Bermuda Inn Fitness and Reducing Resort (CA)	127
Carmel Country Spa (CA)	129
Lakeside Health Resort (CA)	130
Meadowlark Health and Growth Center (CA)	132
Monaco Villa Resort Hotel and Spa (CA)	134
Murrieta Hot Springs Resort, Spa and Conference Center (CA)	136
The Oaks at Ojai (CA)	138
The Palms at Palm Springs (CA)	140
Palm Springs Spa Hotel and Mineral Springs (CA)	142
Weight Watchers at The Surfside Inn (CA)	144

AFFORDABLE SPAS

Wilbur Hot Springs Health Sanctuary (CA)	146
Zane Haven (CA)	147
The Aspen Club (CO)	149
Mountain Meadows Center (CO)	152
Rocky Mountain Wellness Spa (CO)	153
Vail Hotel and Athletic Club (CO)	156
Kalani Honua Intercultural Retreat and Conference Center (HI)	157
Break Away Total Health and Fitness Resort (ID)	159
MGM Desert Inn Hotel and Casino (NV)	161
The Cliff Spa (UT)	163
National Institute of Fitness (UT)	165
Rosario Island Resort and Spa (WA)	167

Chapter Six: Weekend Spa Getaways — 173

Chapter Seven: The Spa Suitcase — 181

Glossary — 189

Index — 203

Spas by State — 207

Introduction

Introduction

Spas — Weighing Benefits, Dispelling Myths

Spa vacations are changing the way health-conscious Americans get away from it all. For many of us, vacationing as a sedentary, sunburned beached whale is a thing of the past. Instead, we want to return from vacation feeling invigorated, rejuvenated and maybe even thinner.

But the word "spa" usually conjures up images of expensive retreats that cater to the rich and famous. After all, everyone's read about the extravagant Golden Door. But how about The Wooden Door, The Glass Door or Tucson National Spa?

Contrary to popular belief, spas don't have to cost a fortune. In fact, most spas are far more affordable than many people realize. Nearly 90 percent of spas now operating in the United States cost less than $1,000 a week. And some are priced in the $400 to $500 range, a far cry from the $3,500 a week charged by some of the well-publicized "super spas."

Another spa myth to dispel concerns clientele. Once the domain of affluent homemakers, spas have shed their "fat farm," idle-rich image. Spas have evolved into well-rounded fitness and health retreats that attract ever-grow-

AFFORDABLE SPAS

ing numbers of professional men and women, families, couples, senior citizens, singles — people from all walks of life who are concerned with health and fitness.

The exciting new breed of "affordable" spas also offers geographical diversity. One can choose a spa in the city or country, desert or mountains, along the coast, in the tropics or on an island.

An Insider's Look

Whether you're looking for a rustic retreat with Shaker-style simplicity or an elegant urban spa with chintz and marble, there's a spa to suit every taste and budget.

Affordable Spas and Fitness Resorts offers spa-goers choices...more than 80 of them. Most of the spas listed in this book cost less than $1,000 a week, with a few priced between $1,000 and $1,150.

Although they cost only a fraction of what super spas cost, many offer the same services, programs and results as their higher-priced counterparts.

A special weekend section includes listings of spas that offer one- or two-night packages, often a good introduction for first-time spa-goers or a quick getaway for fitness-minded professionals.

Price Guide

Dollar signs listed next to each spa in Chapters Two through Six indicate a maximum price per person for three meals a day, double-occupancy accommodations, including some spa services and activities.

Weekend (two nights)	Week-long (six nights)
$ = maximum of $200	maximum of $600
$$ = maximum of $300	maximum of $800
$$$ = maximum of $400	maximum of $1,150

INTRODUCTION

Needless to say, the price ranges in this book are subject to fluctuation. Spas change their rates almost as frequently as the airlines.

Most spas have an additional charge for personal services such as massages, facials and body wraps. Those services cost between $20 and $45 (plus the expected 15 percent tip). Exercise classes and lectures are usually included in the package price. Sometimes private fitness and nutritional counseling costs extra. Always ask what's *not* included in the package price so you get a realistic picture of total costs.

The difference between a $ spa and a $$$ spa is like the difference between a one-star hotel and a three-star hotel. Accommodations vary from luxuriously decorated rooms to rustic cabins with bunk beds. At a $ spa, you might eat at a picnic table in a hall; at a $$$ spa, you might eat on china in a formal dining room. At a $ spa, the staff/guest ratio sometimes isn't as high as it is at a $$$ spa.

Some expensive spas, such as the Palm-Aire in Florida (Elizabeth Taylor's favorite), offer off-season rates. Not only can you experience a $$$$ spa at $$$ rates, but you can do so when the spa isn't crowded, which means more attention from the staff. One of the major advantages of off-season spa travel is the service.

Not all spas with off-season rates are located in areas with uncomfortable weather. The Rocky Mountain region, one of the country's most enjoyable year-round vacation areas, offers off-season rates during the temperate summer and fall seasons. Although Colorado's Aspen Club and Vail Athletic Club and Utah's Cliff Spa are expensive during the ski season, their off-season rates met the affordable pricing standards used in *Affordable Spas and Fitness Resorts.*

When calling a spa about prices, you might not get the same information from one day to the next. That's particularly true of resort spas, which constantly offer specials. To get the best value, it's always wise to call the spa of your choice several times before making reservations.

Some spas offer discounts if you bring a friend or if you're a repeat visitor. Also inquire about special packages

AFFORDABLE SPAS

—weekend specials, holiday specials, even discounts on certain airlines. It pays to call around and check prices.

CHAPTER 1

Anatomy of a Spa

1

What Exactly Is a Spa?

A spa is a resort or hotel with a mineral spring, according to Webster's. But that definition doesn't begin to express the diversity of activities and services typically found at today's spas. They come in all shapes and sizes — from resorts and inns to mountain retreats and city hotels. Most offer a broad range of fitness activities, low-calorie cuisine, and stress reduction, relaxation and beauty treatments.

Some spas emphasize fitness activities more than beauty treatments or stress reduction techniques more than nutritional counseling. Each spa is unique. For instance, The Heartland in Illinois focuses on stress reduction, fitness and health education more than dieting, even though its hearty low-calorie country cuisine often results in weight loss.

Dieting gets top billing at some spas, such as Pawling Health Manor in New York. Others like Kripalu in Massachusetts aren't spas in the traditional sense but rather New Age educational centers offering programs on a wide range of alternative subjects, including holistic health, fitness, nutrition and behavior modification.

Resort Spas vs. Standard Spas

Most spas fall into two categories: *resort spas* — resorts or hotels with a spa on the premises — and what are referred to as *standard spas*, establishments devoted exclusively to diet, fitness and stress reduction. Both classifications have distinct advantages and disadvantages, depending upon your personal interests.

Resort spas are ideal for families or couples who don't have the same vacation goals in mind. One person can sign up for the spa program while the other pursues traditional resort activities. Or guests can combine recreational and spa activities, enjoying the best of both. Most resort spas are full-service hotels with room service, restaurants, boutiques, newsstands and other features.

For those who are serious about losing weight and developing an exercise program, it's not as easy to accomplish those goals at a resort spa because of the many temptations and distractions.

For example, most resort spas serve low-calorie cuisine in the same restaurant where regular food is served. It's hard to nibble contently on carrot curls while the guests at the next table feast on steak, french fries and ice cream. It's up to the individual guest to request low-calorie spa cuisine at most resort spas.

At a standard spa, only low-calorie cuisine is served — hereby avoiding the torture experienced by those counting calories at a resort spa. No one cheats because high-calorie food is nowhere in sight. Alcohol and caffeinated coffee are rarely available.

The cuisine served at most standard spas usually limits guests to a specific calorie count — from 750 to 1,200 calories a day. Portions aren't big. Most guests are hungry during the first few days; after that, the hunger pangs tend to subside.

Most spas do justice to diet food. Nouvelle cuisine, the best thing that ever happened to dieting, has found a niche with many spas. But not all spa food is inventive enough to be called nouvelle or just plain good. A few spas (usually the holistic ones) serve vegetarian cuisine, circa 1972 (tofu burgers and veggie stir-fry). Some spas (usually those catering to senior citizens) serve diet food, circa 1950 (Jell-o and cottage cheese).

If food means a lot to you — and it can become very important when you're limited to 750 calories a day — ask the spa you're interested in to read the day's menu over the phone. Don't rely on brochures; they can make anything sound good.

Standard spa accommodations also tend to be simpler than those found at the resort spas. Often, rooms aren't equipped with phones, televisions or other modern-day distractions. Everyone focuses 100 percent on the spa program. Guests usually rise at the same time (7 or 8 AM) and retire between 9 and 10 PM. At a resort spa you wake up and retire when you feel like it.

All spas offer a wide range of daily activities from which to choose. Most of the spas included in this book do not have a policy of mandatory participation (unlike some of the super spas).

The majority of spas can accommodate between 10 and 30 guests. Because the groups are relatively small, guests usually become friendly with each other. The camaraderie inspires everyone to keep up the good work.

One of the highlights of a week-long spa visit is the end-of-the-week session where guests are weighed and measured. Losing five to seven pounds and a few inches is common. Guests are as elated by the accomplishments of their fellow spa-goers as they are by their own.

The instructors at most spas are excellent, highly trained, better educated and far more supportive than the "bodies beautiful" at many health clubs. Most staff members keep up with the latest fitness, nutrition and diet findings. They're informative and sensitive to guests' concerns. They go to great lengths to keep people from feeling embarrassed or incompetent, no matter how overweight or out of shape guests are. In fact, they inspire confidence. A week at a spa, even a weekend, is a great morale booster.

Of Muscle and Mud — A Day at the Spa

Most spas offer a mind-boggling array of services and programs, usually far too many to expect to take advantage of in a week, let alone a day.

Here are just a few of the services and programs many spas offer: individualized diet and exercise analysis; nutritional counseling; aerobics; body conditioning; yoga; fitness analysis; muscle strengthening; weight lifting; massage; lectures on nutrition, stress reduction, time management, personal wellness and dieting; low-calorie cooking classes; a plethora of relaxation and beauty treatments ranging from herbal wraps, seaweed wraps, mud facials, hair and scalp treatments and skin analysis, to pedicures and manicures. And many include traditional athletics, such as jogging, volleyball, tennis, hiking, golf and swimming.

Some spas are staffed by physicians or nurses and occasionally a psychologist. Staffs often include nutritionists, dieticians, masseuses and masseurs, herbalists, physical therapists, gourmet chefs and physical instructors who all work together to ensure that guests don't overdo or underdo anything — from eating to stretching.

Life after a Spa

But can a spa really make a difference in your life? That depends on how realistic you are and how well you know yourself. After a week at a spa, most people feel a tremendous urge to change many things.

You might go home to your kitchen and think, "I've got to throw everything out: cheese has too much fat; forget about sugar; coffee's no good either." You start reading labels (a lot of spas teach you how to do this) and discover the so-called light brands you're using are loaded with nutritional saboteurs.

If you aren't already involved in a regular exercise program, you may be eager to sign up for classes right away or buy an exercise bicycle. The urge to completely reform is powerful and unrealistic.

ANATOMY OF A SPA

Most spas suggest that guests change one thing. Take a walk every other day. Eliminate cheese from your diet. Do yoga in the morning if you need to relax. You can't change everything. Adding one activity a day or altering your eating habits can make an enormous difference in your health.

A spa visit makes you more aware of your general well-being—how much exercise you get, how you handle stress, what you eat. Awareness is half the battle. A lot of people go back to a favorite spa twice a year to rekindle their interest and learn more.

CHAPTER 2

Northeastern Spas and Fitness Resorts

2

CONNECTICUT

GRAND LAKE SPA HOTEL

Lebanon, Connecticut

$ and $$
Open: Year-round

This is the spa for anyone on a budget who wants to lose weight and/or hasn't exercised much. Grand Lake offers an excellent fitness and weight loss program that produces the same results as the super spas for a fraction of the price. (Most guests at Grand Lake shed between seven and ten pounds a week.)

Upon arrival, guests are given a private fitness evaluation and physical by the spa's registered nurse. She then recommends a nutrition and exercise program, based on personal needs and goals.

Although specific classes are recommended, the choice is entirely up to the individual. Throughout the day, guests can participate in a wide range of activities and services, such as aerobics, yoga, stress management seminars and massage.

AFFORDABLE SPAS

Grand Lake offers daily rates and three-day, midweek, four-day and seven-day packages. It also features two special tests (not included in the spa package price): "Computerized Body Composition Analysis" ($30) and "The Blood Chemistry Test" ($50). The former calculates the body's fat, muscle and fluid content. Based on that information, the computer then determines a recommended caloric intake, estimated weight loss over a certain period of time and probable caloric expenditures for approximately 30 different activities.

"The Blood Chemistry Test" determines cholesterol, triglyceride and glucose levels. A nurse analyzes the results.

Located on a lake in central Connecticut, Grand Lake Spa is a comfortable, moderately priced spa in a serene setting. It boasts lush flower gardens and rolling meadows.

Eighty-five percent of Grand Lake guests are women 18 and older who are serious about weight loss. The spa's supportive staff also makes it an ideal place for people who've never exercised much and feel intimidated by the thought of aerobics.

Activities & Services

Low-impact aerobics and other exercise classes, yoga, walking, swimming, Swedish and shiatsu massage, swimnastics, stress management seminars, nutritional counseling and lectures, personalized style and color analysis, facials, manicures, pedicures, full-service beauty salon, hot tub, sauna, whirlpool, tennis.

Lodging

Standard and deluxe rooms are comfortable and simple. The atmosphere is quaint and casual.

Cuisine

Guests can choose a daily 650-, 900- or 1,200-calorie diet. Those who prefer not to diet can eat as much of the low-calorie food as they want. Most opt for the 650-calorie plan. Sample dishes are artichoke pasta primavera, marinated mushroom salad, chicken breast basted in orange glaze and broiled Gulf shrimp.

Grand Lake Spa Hotel	203-642-6696
Route 207	800-237-2772(CT)
Lebanon, CT 06249	800-232-2772 (out of state, in northeastern U.S.)

NORWICH INN AND SPA

Norwich, Connecticut

$$$
Open: Year-round

Norwich Inn calls itself "the lowest priced luxury resort in the country." Featuring beautiful guest rooms, gourmet dining and some of the luxe touches one would expect to find at a $3,500-a-week spa, the Norwich Inn is owned by the Edward J. Safdie Group, which also owns two well-known super spas: The Greenhouse in Dallas and The California Terrace and Spa in Monte Carlo.

Located in a romantic, red-brick Georgian building surrounded by New England countryside, the Norwich Inn and Spa features state-of-the-art programs and facilities, but the atmosphere is pure country manor. Decorated with antiques, chintz upholstered armchairs and sofas, Chippendale mirrors, rag rugs and ruffled curtains, Norwich has attracted a diverse group of celebrities over the years — Frank Sinatra, George Bernard Shaw, Charles Laughton, even the late Duke of Windsor, before he became king.

Today the spa is a refuge for New York City professionals, who take advantage of the corporate spa package or the popular weekend "Revitalizer" program. The spa also attracts fitness-minded vacationers, drawn to the lovely environment and high-quality programs.

Most guests are more concerned with health, fitness and stress management than with dieting. Even though Norwich is a far cry from a fat farm, most guests still manage to lose three to five pounds a week.

One of Norwich's biggest pluses is the staff/guest ratio—one-to-one. Before arriving, guests are asked to complete a questionnaire. A fitness evaluation, conducted upon arrival, and the completed questionnaire enable the staff to design a program appropriate to each guest's individual goals and abilities.

Activities & Services

"The Connecticut Workout" (low-impact, high-energy exercises), aquacise, power play (a monitored workout with Keiser Cam II weight equipment), limber and tone, body awareness (for posture and body alignment), yoga, T'ai Chi, fitness evaluation, body composition, nutritional counseling (costs $40 and requires 48-hour notice), facials, massage, aromatherapy, hydrotherapy, body scrub, thalassotherapy seaweed wrap, hand and foot treatments, neck and shoulder massage, makeup consultation, evening seminars on health and fitness subjects, sauna, steam room, whirlpool, swimming, golf, tennis.

Lodging

Each of the 65 rooms is unique. Some have antique four-poster beds that are so high a foot stool is needed to climb in and out of them. One room has an Adirondack-style twig bed (which sounds uncomfortable, but isn't). All rooms have quaint touches, such as colorful quilts and country print wallpaper.

Cuisine

1,200, 1,500 or 1,800 calories a day are served in the spa dining room. The chef takes full advantage of the bountiful local produce. Many low-calorie, Yankee-inspired dishes are featured: seafood sausage, poached pears, fruit sorbet and baked apple, to name a few.

NORTHEASTERN SPAS

Norwich Inn and Spa
Route 32
Norwich, CT 06360

203-886-2401
800-892-5692

WEIGHT WATCHERS AT THE HARTFORD TREADWAY HOTEL

Cromwell, Connecticut

$$

Open: Year-round

There's so much to do and see in this part of New England that guests feel more like they're on vacation than at a weight loss resort. They can visit Old Mystic Village, Yale and Wesleyan universities, Mark Twain's home in Hartford and Harriet Beecher Stowe's home in New Haven. Or they can explore art galleries, museums and antique shops in quaint New England towns.

In between sight-seeing activities, they manage to lose a considerable amount of weight by participating in The Hartford Treadway Hotel's spa program, run by Weight Watchers. The program includes daily exercise classes, motivational workshops and lectures, and beauty and relaxation treatments.

Weight Watchers is realistic about exercise. Guests are encouraged to participate in fitness activities they're likely to continue at home, instead of exercises they won't bother to do again.

Much time is devoted to learning how to increase willpower, control stress, keep weight loss motivation high and assert oneself. Group support is a key element to the program. Guests are encouraged to help each other, and they do.

A typical day's schedule might begin with a morning stretch class, a walk before breakfast, a stretch and tone (flexercise) class, aerobics and water exercises. After lunch, activities might include a workshop, a massage or yoga.

■ AFFORDABLE SPAS

After dinner, guests can enjoy evening entertainment in the Treadway's piano lounge and nightclub.

Activities & Services

Aerobics, aquacise, stretch and tone, yoga, Nautilus and Universal exercise equipment, lectures and workshops on behavior modification, personal exercise program, nutritional counseling, group support sessions, massage, sauna, whirlpool, walks, swimming, golf, tennis, skiing.

Lodging

Guest rooms are tastefully decorated. Special touches include morning newspaper delivery, nightly turn-down bed service and personalized wake-up calls.

Cuisine

1,000 calories a day. Sample dishes are red snapper with sesame vegetables, linguine with bay scallops and honeyed pumpkin custard.

The Hartford Treadway Hotel
100 Berlin Road
Cromwell, CT 06416

For more information on Weight Watchers program at The Hartford Treadway and its other programs, contact

Weight Watchers Resorts and Spas   313-443-1414
15815 W. 12 Mile Road   800-LEANER-U
Southfield, MI 48076   800-826-5088 (Canada)

MAINE

NORTHERN PINES HEALTH RESORT

Raymond, Maine

$

Open: May to November;
January to April

This 80-acre lakeside health retreat offers an excellent diet and fitness program. Although most resorts in cold climates close during the winter, Northern Pines reopens in January, taking advantage of all the good things winter has to offer.

Its winter spa program includes cross-country skiing, walks through the woods, cozy evening lectures and talks in front of the fireplace. In addition, exercising and dieting in cold weather often results in greater weight loss than in warm weather because the body works harder to maintain body temperature.

Northern Pines is a good choice for anyone who enjoys cold climate sports and winter wonderland scenery. It attracts far more men (65 percent) than women at that time of year. (During the summer, the percentages are reversed.) This makes it a popular winter spa for singles. "We've had a few weddings between guests who met here," says Spa Manager Doris Resnick. Few health retreats can claim such promising odds for single women.

Guests include many professionals, winter and summer. Summer clientele also includes a healthy percentage of nonprofessional women over 40.

The primary objective of Northern Pines' diet and fitness program isn't quick weight loss, but rather to teach guests how to lead healthier lives. "This is not a fat farm where weight loss is accomplished in a quick way," explains Resnick. "We take a more relaxed, holistic approach, so it lasts. Developing a healthier lifestyle is a slow transition."

AFFORDABLE SPAS

Upon arrival, a guest's fitness level and weight loss goals are determined. An instructor then recommends certain exercise classes based on an individual's abilities. Four different supervised exercise programs operate daily — everything from aerobics and body conditioning to hiking and cross-country skiing. The staff also will develop a personalized diet/exercise regimen upon request.

Most guests prefer an unstructured program. They can participate in as many or as few exercise classes as they choose. "Some guests just sit in a hammock all day and read," says Resnick. "You have a lot of freedom."

In addition to exercise classes, personal services such as massage are also offered, as are two daily health-related lectures and discussions.

Trips are sometimes planned to nearby areas of interest, such as the L. L. Bean store in Freeport, the White Mountains, the Saco River and Portland. Northern Pines is about a two-and-a-half-hour drive from Boston and a 45-minute drive from Portland.

Activities & Services

Stretching, walks, yoga, aerobics, body conditioning, hiking, massage, facials, reflexology, hair treatments, body work, shoulder massage. Classes in nutrition, stress management, weight control and other health-related topics. Swimming, hot tub, sauna, pedal boat, sailing, cross-country skiing.

Lodging

Beautifully restored lakeside log cabins (circa 1920), some with fireplaces, are available. However, they have shared bathroom facilities. The Hillside and Yurt rooms, designed to blend in with the older cabins, also have shared bathrooms. The Cedar and Pine rooms have private baths.

Cuisine

The vegetarian diet cuisine, limited to 800 calories a day, includes Mexican, Middle Eastern and Japanese dishes in addition to dishes such as pasta and vegetable Stroganoff. A fasting program is available. It includes two days of raw fresh fruits and vegetables prior to the fast, followed by three days of transition. Fasting juices include fresh fruit, vegetable juices and broth. Also offered is a raw vegetable and fruit diet, which many guests choose over fasting because the resulting weight loss is about the same and easier to maintain.

Northern Pines Health Resort
Rural Route 1
Box 279   207-655-7624
Raymond, Maine 04071   212-255-4864 (New York City)

MASSACHUSETTS

EVERNEW SUMMER SPA CAMP FOR WOMEN

$$

Milton Village, Massachusetts   Open: July and August

Finding most spas either too luxurious and expensive or too rustic, Barbara Slater decided to open one that fit nicely in between. In 1984, she started Evernew, a spa for women that operates for six weeks every summer at Mount Holyoke College.

"Our goal is to give women a gentle yet persuasive nudge toward a healthier lifestyle," says Slater, a former attorney and television producer.

The spa attracts many well-educated professional women. More than half the guests want to lose weight; the others are already in good shape.

AFFORDABLE SPAS

The spa offers a five-day exercise, diet and beauty program. A diversity of exercise classes and educational workshops is scheduled daily. Among the most popular are wardrobe planning, expanding creative solutions and dealing with stress.

The diet plan is refreshing and realistic. "We all know diets don't work," comments Slater. "We offer a healthy menu that is low in fat, sugar, salt and cholesterol—one that is easy to continue at home. After all, eating is just a habit, and one we can change."

The diet isn't designed for quick weight loss, but rather to reduce fat intake and thus help guests become healthier. A personalized fitness and diet program is also available upon request.

The tranquil Mount Holyoke campus occupies 800 acres of New England countryside—rolling hills, lakes, forests, brooks and waterfalls.

Activities & Services

Low- and high-impact aerobics, conditioning, stretch and relaxation, race walking, aquacise, yoga, massage, facials, manicures, pedicures, makeup and color analysis, sauna, tennis, swimming, golf, horseback riding, bicycling, squash, racquetball. Workshops on nutrition, skincare and makeup, figure analysis, wardrobe planning, massage techniques, stress management.

Lodging

Guests stay in Mount Holyoke dormitory rooms. Single and double rooms with private baths are available.

Cuisine

1,200 calories a day. Sample dishes are French toast with berries, vegetable cheese custard pie and tandoori chicken with saffron rice.

Evernew Summer Camp for Women
P.O. Box 183
Milton Village, MA 02187   617-265-7756

KRIPALU CENTER

Lenox, Massachusetts

$ and $$
Open: Year-round

Kripalu (pronounced kri-pah-loo) is the quintessential holistic health retreat. The nonprofit, volunteer organization, named for yoga master Swami Shri Kripalvanandji, offers programs on personal growth, yoga, spiritual attunement, health, fitness and body work.

Kripalu also offers acceptance — complete acceptance of the individual no matter how out of shape or out of touch he or she is. It's very much in keeping with the underlying theme of Kripalu Center's programs: Learn to love thyself.

This is *not* the kind of place that rewards the highest leg lifts. Weight loss and competitive fitness aren't common goals at Kripalu. Instead, the focus is on one's overall health and feelings about oneself.

Kripalu's approach to physical and emotional health incorporates Eastern spiritual beliefs and Western psychological techniques. The staff is caring and committed to the center's principles. People who are ill at ease about opening up both heart and mind to caring strangers may not be comfortable here. Those who are able to discuss their feelings openly will find a supportive environment.

Guests can visit Kripalu for a day, weekend, week or longer. They can take individual classes or sign up for special programs. Kripalu's "Anytime" program is a potpourri of activities such as guided meditation, wake-up walks, yoga, workshops on such subjects as health and communication, aerobic dance and more.

Numerous other weekend, week-long and month-long programs are available at specific times of the year, in-

AFFORDABLE SPAS

cluding "Welcome Weekend," which includes yoga, self-awareness workshops, creative movement and spiritual attunement; and "High Energy Living: Recharging Your Vitality," a program based on Hara Kinetics, an invigorating experience that focuses on movements reminiscent of the martial arts. Children's programs also are available.

Located in the Berkshires near Tanglewood (summer home of the Boston Symphony Orchestra), Kripalu Center occupies 350 acres of sunlit forests, meadows, a lake and countless walking trails.

Kripalu guests often explore the area's many cultural and scenic attractions. Two quaint New England villages, Stockbridge (of Norman Rockwell fame) and Lenox, offer good antique shopping and interesting historical tours.

The clientele at Kripalu tends to run the gamut from the quiet and spiritual to professionals wanting to relax. It draws a slightly higher percentage of women than men.

Activities & Services

Many activities depend upon the specific program. However, the center also offers activities year-round. They include body work, polarity therapy, yoga, shiatsu, reflexology, facial skincare (using excellent natural skincare products available for purchase), flotation tank, personal counseling (relationships, career decisions, lifestyle reevaluation, health status or spiritual growth), guided meditation, nature walks, DansKinetics (aerobic exercises with yogic-based stretches), holistic health workshops, lake swimming, hiking, whirlpool, sauna.

Lodging

Accommodations range from camplike dorms with ten to 22 bunk beds and shared bathrooms to private double rooms with bathrooms. Guests rent or bring their own sheets, blankets and towels. Some guests stay at nearby inns and use the center during the day.

Cuisine

There is no diet program. The vegetarian menu is based on an abundance of fresh, natural foods — homemade breads, soups, generous salad bar and vegetarian entrees (such as tofu kabobs and pasta dishes).

Kripalu Center
Box 793
Lenox, MA 01240   413-637-3280

NEW JERSEY

THE SPA AT BALLY'S

Atlantic City, New Jersey

$$ and $$$
Open: Year-round

Located in one of Atlantic City's casino hotels, The Spa at Bally's epitomizes super-spa elegance, but at moderate prices. Whether guests are serious spa-goers or in need of a respite from the hotel's casino, people can shape up or calm down in the lap of luxury.

The multitiered Coral Whirlpool Park is the spa's popular "wet area," a cavernous atrium with a pool, hot tubs and mosaic Jacuzzis, surrounded by lush plants, exotic flowers, waterfalls and fountains. After a swim and a visit to the ornately tiled Turkish steam room or the glass-enclosed sauna, spa-goers can lounge on the sun deck overlooking Atlantic City's famous Boardwalk. The high-tech design, palette of soft colors and beautiful tile work blend together to give the spa a fresh, airy feeling.

Guests also can take advantage of Bally's special two-night or five-night spa packages (approximately $400 and $800 respectively), which include double occupancy accommodations, calorie-controlled meals and a number of classes and relaxation services such as massage.

AFFORDABLE SPAS

Activities & Services

Aquacise, low-impact aerobics, free dance, yoga, slimnastics, relaxation and stretch, controlled aerobics, Swedish and shiatsu massage, loofah scrub, salt glow loofah, body cleansing loofah, herbal wrap, aromatherapy wrap, facial, whirlpool, sauna, hot tubs, Jacuzzis, Swiss showers, swimming, tanning room, Nautilus equipment, diet and lifestyle modification lectures, health consultations.

Lodging

Guests stay in Bally's Park Place Casino Hotel, which also houses The Spa at Bally's. Accommodations range from standard, double-occupancy rooms to deluxe rooms, some of which are appointed with round beds and sunken tubs. (Deluxe rooms are limited and must be specially requested.) All rooms are stocked with toiletries.

Cuisine

Open from 11:30 AM to 4 PM daily, the Spa Cafe serves low-cholesterol food. Entrees include California warm chicken salad, all egg-white omelette with tomatoes and mushrooms, and turkey burgers. It also has a full-service bar, which in addition to alcoholic beverages mixes delicious nonalcoholic fruit drinks.

The Spa at Bally's
Bally's Park Place Casino Hotel
Park Place and Boardwalk　　　　　609-340-4600
Atlantic City, NJ 08401　　　　　　800-772-7777

HARBOR ISLAND SPA

West End, New Jersey

$ and $$
Open: Year-round

Harbor Island attracts spa-goers who want to lose weight, have a good time and pay a reasonable price ($500 to $600 for six nights, double occupancy, all meals and activities). It's ideal for anyone over 40 who wants to start an exercise and diet program or revive one that has lapsed. Most guests at this high-rise, beachfront spa are women.

A dietician and fitness instructor work with each guest to develop a personalized diet and exercise regimen.

All activities are voluntary. The morning schedule begins with an 8:40 AM walk followed by slow, easy stretches, light exercises and yoga. Afternoons feature instruction on weight equipment, wand exercises (former drum majorettes love this one) and additional exercise classes. Relaxation and beauty activities such as reflexology and body wraps are offered throughout the day.

Most spas consider nightlife to be an affliction; Harbor Island breaks the mold. Forget mock cocktails. At Harbor Island, guests get the real thing.

Live music, shows and dinner dancing enliven the evenings, along with sing-alongs, bingo and card games. On Saturday nights, many guests put on the Ritz, in honor of Harbor Island Spa's weekly champagne cocktail hour.

Activities & Services

Aerobics, aquacise, stretching, calisthenics, yoga, wand exercises, walks, light gymnastics, massage, facials, body wraps, reflexology, saunas, whirlpools, steam rooms, swimming, gym, tennis, golf, racquetball, handball, full-service beauty salon.

◾ AFFORDABLE SPAS

Lodging

Accommodations are comfortable and inviting. Guests stay in newly renovated hotel rooms in the original building or in the newly constructed wings.

Cuisine

Diet and nondiet food is served. Calorie count depends on the individual, who consults with the dietician to determine average daily calorie intake. Sample dishes from the diet menu are vegetable cutlet, grilled fresh fish and vegetables.

Harbor Island Spa
701 Ocean Avenue   201-222-2600 (NJ)
West End, NJ 07740   212-406-1162 (NY)

MAYFAIR: THE SPA BY THE SEA

Ventnor, New Jersey

$$ and $$$
Open: Year-round

By the age of 52, Shirley Weiner had tried every diet imaginable. But it was the same old story: Nothing worked. So she called a halt to the dieting madness and decided, "If I'm destined to be a fat person, then at least I can eat well."

Weiner started eating healthy food without paying much attention to calories and, much to her surprise, lost weight. That experience inspired her to open Mayfair, her own weight loss spa utilizing the same formula that worked for her.

Weiner's philosophy: Fad diets don't work; good eating habits, combined with a minimal amount of daily exercise, do.

Located two miles from Atlantic City, the spa occupies a meticulously restored 1920s beachfront house decorated in period furnishings, antique wicker and flowered chintz.

Guests at Mayfair are serious about weight loss. It's popular with businesswomen, senior citizens and homemakers. Some guests are noticeably overweight; others want to lose five to ten pounds, which most patrons do after a week here.

The atmosphere is casual and friendly, the pace leisurely but not lazy. The spa offers a structured exercise program with a variety of classes so guests get more than enough in the way of fitness activities.

The daily schedule of voluntary activities usually includes a walk or bicycle ride on the beach or boardwalk before breakfast. After breakfast, guests can participate in dancercise, light weight workout, stretching and rubber-band resistant exercises. The afternoon often features a massage, whirlpool, dry heat sauna and facial.

Informal behavior modification classes are taught throughout the day. Individual nutritional counseling is available. Evening seminars focus on subjects such as the psychology of the diet craze in America.

The spa offers two special packages: the seven-day "Elegant Boot Camp" and the four-day (Thursday through Sunday) "Executive Women's Mini-Boot Camp."

The spa is very strict about cheating—junk food, caffeinated drinks, alcohol and cigarettes are strictly verboten.

Activities & Services

Nutritional and behavior modification counseling, stretch and strengthen exercises, dance and body movement, walking, soft aerobics, yoga, whirlpool, sauna, Jacuzzi, massage, herbal wrap, facial, lectures, instructive videos.

Lodging

Guest rooms are light, airy and attractively decorated. Single, double and triple rooms are priced accordingly.

AFFORDABLE SPAS

Cuisine

800 to 1,000 calories a day. Guest don't even think about sneaking down the boardwalk for a slice of pizza. "We always find out," says Weiner. The chef prepares a menu based on ethnic dishes and high fiber without using any dairy, pork or red meat.

Mayfair: The Spa by the Sea
105 S. Little Rock Avenue
Ventnor, NJ 08406 609-487-8083

THE SHOREHAM HOTEL

$$
Spring Lake, New Jersey Open: Year-round

This stately turn-of-the-century Victorian hotel harkens back to an era when recreational activities consisted of lawn croquet and tennis. Today The Shoreham Hotel offers a lot more, but still maintains the feeling of a grand old hotel.

The Shoreham features a fairly unique program that tends to attract active, fun-loving people over 40. Such activities as poolside ballroom dancing, Dixieland bands, fashion shows (one by furrier Antonovich) and scavenger hunts are offered, in addition to exercise classes, stress reduction activities and beauty treatments.

With the ocean on one side of the hotel and a lake on the other, guests feel like they're on a cruise ship. The activities and the enthusiastic staff further contribute to the cruise-ship ambience.

Some of The Shoreham's guests are serious about dieting and working out; others are there to have a good time. It's an ideal retreat for couples with different interests and vacation goals.

NORTHEASTERN SPAS

The hotel is located a block away from a two-mile non-commerical boardwalk that is popular with guests for strolling, jogging or just relaxing.

Activities & Services

Low-impact aerobics, front porch chair exercises (good for semi-mobile guests), aquacise, stress management lectures, massage (Swedish, sports and therapeutic), herbal body wraps, facials, makeup demonstrations, makeovers, bicycling, swimming, personalized fitness program, manicures, pedicures. Nearby golf, tennis, sailing and deep-sea fishing. Live bands, Sunday champagne brunch, luaus, barbecues, films, Atlantic City outings and yacht cruises.

Lodging

Guest rooms reflect the period of the hotel. Each one is furnished uniquely and some have lake views.

Cuisine

Low-calorie and nondiet dishes are served in the same dining room. Samples from the diet menu (no set calorie count) include broiled swordfish, *sole en papiotte*, dilled shrimp. Nondiet dishes include swordfish with honey raisin sauce, grilled steak with butter and chicken stuffed with proscuitto wrapped in bacon.

The Shoreham Hotel
Box 225-115
Spring Lake, NJ 07762   201-449-7100

■ AFFORDABLE SPAS

NEW YORK

LIVING SPRINGS RETREAT

Putnam Valley, New York $$

Open: Year-round

    Located in the Berkshire Mountains, an hour north of New York City, Living Springs Retreat is a health reconditioning center for people who have special health needs.

    The goal here is to prevent or combat "lifestyle diseases," such as high blood pressure, heart disease, diabetes and hypoglycemia, all the while maintaining health, vitality and longevity.

    Living Springs seeks to integrate the mind, body and spirit. Guests are provided with the support needed to overcome health-related problems. A five-day smoking cessation program helps guests through withdrawal with contrast water baths (used to stimulate the body's natural healing processes) and emotional and spiritual support. The stress control program features techniques that help guests break the cycle of anxiety and frustration.

    Although there's no emphasis on intense weight reduction, the retreat's holistic approach to weight management provides a wholesome program of diet and exercise. Fad diets and drug treatment for obesity are strictly forbidden here. Counseling is offered in meal planning, nutrition and coping with food weaknesses.

    The physical conditioning program is designed around personalized daily exercises, followed by a long-term, progressive plan that allows guests to reach their highest level of fitness.

    Living Springs Retreat is run in cooperation with Community Health Services of Seventh-Day Adventists. The retreat's program, however, is nondenominational, and people of all religions are welcome.

Activities & Services

Guided exercise. Programs on stress, nutrition and weight, smoking cessation. Hydrotherapy demonstrations, walks, whirlpool, steam bath, sauna. Health lectures, videos and slide programs. Cooking classes, medical consultations (for an extra fee).

Lodging

Private and shared rooms, some with lake views, are housed in a quaintly furnished lodge. The main parlor has a stone fireplace.

Cuisine

Vegetarian holistic cuisine is served buffet-style. The food is plentiful. However, guests on the weight management program are offered lower calorie cuisine. Picnic lunches full of fresh fruit and vegetables are available.

Living Springs Retreat
Route 3, Box 357
Putnam Valley, NY 10579   914-526-2800

MOHONK MOUNTAIN HOUSE

New Paltz, New York

$$$
Open: Year-round

The long, winding road leading to this Shawangunk Mountain resort is completely surrounded by woods. Suddenly, a 300-room mansion appears out of nowhere, like something out of a dream.

It is Mohonk Mountain House, with its eclectic appointment of turrets, towers, gables, porches and gingerbread. Nothing seems to have changed at this estate,

AFFORDABLE SPAS

which combines Adirondack, Victorian and Edwardian architecture, since it was built in the late 1800s. One expects Teddy Roosevelt and his Rough Riders to come charging up the road any minute.

It's not surprising to learn that a couple of years ago Neiman-Marcus featured a weekend at the Mohonk Mountain House as a gift item in its Christmas catalog. It's a very special place.

A grand, sweeping veranda lined with Adirondack-style rocking chairs overlooks Mohonk Lake, which is surrounded by mountains, forest and huge rock formations. The view is so mesmerizing, guests have been known to plant themselves in a rocker and not move for days.

The gardens are a work of art, producing fresh flowers for the resort's many parlors and drawing rooms. The estate is also crisscrossed by 135 miles of walking trails, which have twig benches and gazebos located at scenic points.

Mohonk isn't a spa or health retreat, but rather a resort that features daily activities and theme weekends, some of which are health- and fitness-oriented. Among the popular health programs, hosted by experts in that particular field, are "Stress Management and Maintaining Wellness," "Running and Fitness" and "Walking for Health."

The stress management weekend includes learning how to create a stress-free diet and exercise program, take charge of your schedule, use affirmation and visualization techniques for peak performance and health, meditate for relaxing and revitalizing, and employ deep relaxation techniques for relieving physical and mental tension. Needless to say, working people are well represented at this seminar.

The "Running and Fitness" weekend offers a physical fitness profile that is personalized and trainer-assisted and includes blood pressure check, body fat assessment, flexibility test and heart-rate training range. Also featured are aerobics, stretching, fun runs, a running tour of Mohonk's grounds, evening and afternoon lectures and roundtable discussions with running and fitness experts. The Great Race, held Sunday morning, is described by *Sports Illustrated* as "the world's most beautiful."

NORTHEASTERN SPAS

The "Walking for Health" weekend, still being developed at the time of this writing, promises to be quite special, given the beautiful setting. It will include some of the activities offered in the "Running and Fitness" weekend.

Mohonk also offers clever theme weeks and weekends unrelated to health and fitness, such as the popular "Mystery Weekend," "Birding and Nature," "Science Fiction Weekend" and "Hiker's Holiday."

Guests can visit Mohonk for the day, the weekend or longer to simply enjoy the resort without participating in theme activities.

The room price may seem steep (from around $192 to $290, for a special tower room), but like prices at a European hotel, it includes three meals a day and most activities and services.

Activities & Services

(Excluding activities described above for special weekends): Stretching, aerobics, weight training, nutrition, heart care classes, sauna, massage, tennis, golf, horseback riding, boating, lake swimming, hiking, summer hayrides, outdoor cookouts, night hikes, campfires, ghost stories, winter cross-country skiing and sleigh rides, music concerts, a multitude of daily seasonal activities.

Lodging

Accommodations comprise rooms with basin only, regular guest rooms and special tower rooms, priced accordingly. Most rooms have views and porches. All are furnished with antiques and reproductions.

Cuisine

Mohonk doesn't serve diet cuisine, but traditional hearty American fare. The beautiful main dining room boasts spectacular views. Sample dishes are turkey with stuffing and cranberry sauce, braised veal stew with leeks, banana cream pie, pineapple upside down cake. Vegetarian

AFFORDABLE SPAS

and kosher cuisines are available upon request. Liquor is available at dinner in the dining room.

Mohonk Mountain House
Lake Mohonk
New Paltz, NY 12561   914-255-1000

NEW AGE HEALTH FARM

Neversink, New York

$, $$ and $$$
Open: Year-round

Although diet programs are available at New Age Health Farm, many patrons come here for juice fasting. Fasters lose more than just weight. Fasting helps rid the body of toxins as well as negative feelings such as anger, jealousy, despair or grief that have been stored up over the years, according to New Age staff members. Those views aren't unique to New Age. Many proponents believe fasting affects an individual physically, mentally and spiritually.

Most fasters aren't overweight but are interested in detoxifying their systems. They generally lose a pound a day, while dieters lose an average of five pounds a week.

Fasting is just part of the Health Farm's program, which is deeply rooted in holistic health and "New Age" thinking. The primary objective of many New Age guests, most of whom are women, is to learn how to lead a healthier, less hectic life.

Guests can request private consultations with the staff to determine their fitness level and individual diets. An exercise and nutrition plan is also available. A variety of fitness, relaxation and educational activities are offered throughout the day—everything from nature walks and yoga, to calisthenics and lectures on "Learning How to Love Yourself," and "The Psychology of Fasting."

The farm, located in the Catskill Mountains, is a peace

NORTHEASTERN SPAS

ful rural retreat, particularly scenic during the fall when the landscape is rich with color.

In addition to New Age's natural wonders, it offers some beautiful prices. Guests can spend $1,000 for a seven-night stay (single occupancy, including all meals and most services and activities).

Activities & Services

Yoga, meditation, warm-up classes, aquacise, weight training, calisthenics, low-impact aerobics, walks, Swedish and shiatsu massage, reflexology, aromatherapy facial, paraffin body treatment, Dead Sea mud treatment, loofah rub, mud packs, full-service beauty salon, astrology readings, swimming, volleyball, cross-country skiing.

Lodging

Three types of accommodations are available and priced accordingly. The largest and most expensive rooms boast the best views. All rooms have private baths.

Cuisine

A variety of fasts and diet programs are offered. The water fast, the most stringent regimen, requires a doctor's permission. The 350-calorie breaker diet of fruit, salad and vegetables is designed to help ease fasters back into food. Most fasters start this diet right before going home. Also available are 450-, 800-, 1,000- and 1,200-calorie diet programs. Nondieters simply eat as much low-calorie food as they want. Sample dishes from the vegetarian menu are tofu meatballs and tempeh burgers.

New Age Health Farm
Route 55
Neversink, NY 12765

914-985-7601
800-682-4348 (NY)

■ AFFORDABLE SPAS

OMEGA INSTITUTE FOR HOLISTIC STUDIES

Rhinebeck, New York

$

Open: Summer

Omega Institute is like a counterculture summer camp for adults. It offers more than 200 weekend and week-long programs on health, fitness, preventive medicine, psychology, the arts, business, global thinking and spirituality.

Its health and fitness classes are just like those offered at a first-rate holistic spa. The only difference is that at Omega Institute, the programs are taught by preeminent leaders in their fields. Every summer, the institute enlists experts in a wide range of areas to teach courses and workshops. As a result, Omega guests are instructed by the best in the business.

Guests can sign up for the institute's various health and fitness classes on an a la carte basis or participate in a package program for a flat rate, which includes a preselected assortment of classes and workshops.

Two packages described in detail below are the "Wellness Program" and "Fitness Week." The former integrates wellness, fitness, stress management and relaxation. "Fitness Week" emphasizes mind/body relationships, goal-setting, motivational training, muscle conditioning and Eastern body awareness systems.

The institute offers a vast array of courses, such as "Fitness over 50," "The Dance of Tennis," "Breaking Free from Compulsive Eating" and "Tibetan Medicine Training." Also addressed in workshops and courses are such subjects as herbology, psychodrama, releasing addiction, intuition, anger, working with dreams, new frontiers for men, mother/daughter relationships, tap dance, humor, creativity and compassion.

Because most courses at Omega Institute might be labeled as counterculture in nature, one might expect the clientele to be made up of eccentrics and aging hippies. Not so. The institute attracts people of all ages with different interests from all walks of life.

Although Omega Institute offers a course on weight management, it's not the place for people whose primary interest is in losing weight. It doesn't feature a diet plan or official weight loss program. Those who blush at coed nudity might want to avoid the coed sauna.

Located in the Hudson River Valley, the lakeside campus occupies 80 wooded acres. Many classes are taught outdoors in lovely meadow settings.

The atmosphere is educational and friendly. It's a good bet for people who want to expand their minds, experiences and fitness potential.

Omega Institute also offers a "Family Week" with a children's program.

Activities & Services

Below is a detailed description of the "Wellness Program" and "Fitness Week." Omega Institute also offers other classes and packages every summer. (Consult the institute's catalog.)

"The Omega Wellness Program": Lectures on nutrition, vitamins, immune system, personal eating habits, stress and exercise, preventive medicine, how to create one's own wellness program. Aerobic conditioning, stretching and muscle strengthening, stress reduction, meditation, relaxation, massage, yoga, T'ai Chi, group support sessions, body tuning, music, walking, weight management.

"Fitness Week" (offered at beginning and intermediate/advanced levels): Yoga for athletes, Chinese exercises, running, improving cycling efficiency, breathing, swimming, women's fitness, the Tao of the physical.

Lodging

Cabins with shared baths, dormitory accommodations and campsites are available. Guests bring their own soap and towels.

■ AFFORDABLE SPAS

Cuisine

The vegetarian whole food menu includes tofu quiche and artichoke and soy spaghetti. No diet menu is available.

Omega Institute for Holistic Studies
R.D. 2, Box 377　　　　　　　　　　　914-338-6030
Rhinebeck, NY 12572　　　　　(September 16 to May 14)
　　　　　　　　　　　　　　　　　　　914-266-4301
　　　　　　　　　　　　　　　(May 15 to September 15)

LE PARKER MERIDIEN

New York, New York

$$$/Weekends
Open: Year-round

This elegant New York City hotel offers a special spa weekend package that combines big city fun with fitness and gourmet dieting. Those who can tear themselves away from all the shopping in this part of town (e.g., Bloomingdale's, Bergdorf Goodman and Tiffany) can shape up in Le Parker Meridien's Club La Raquette and slim down on French diet cuisine.

Although the hotel provides every spa guest with a suggested itinerary, the choice of activities is up to the individual. No one keeps tabs on who missed the aerobics class. Among the exercise classes offered throughout the day is "Fitness with Finesse," a deep muscle workout for beginners and intermediates with emphasis on strengthening and stretching with free weights.

"Muscle Madness," an intermediate high-energy, fast-paced workout, concentrates on upper and lower extremities, abdomen and buttocks.

Those on a business trip or a schedule that precludes a long workout often choose the "Eat and Run" program, a 30-minute revitalizing wake-up workout and high-energy, low-calorie spa breakfast, designed specifically for execu-

NORTHEASTERN SPAS

tives who want to greet the new day with a roar.

Other activities scheduled throughout the day include fitness walks to different Manhattan neighborhoods, such as SoHo and Wall Street.

Club La Raquette, a penthouse with a pool, Nautilus equipment and outdoor jogging track (weather permitting), boasts a spectacular view of Manhattan. For those who prefer to exercise in the privacy of their own room, the hotel airs an in-room fitness video continuously every day on a closed-circuit system.

Given its location, the hotel attracts quite a few business people and vacationers. However, couples from the city's suburban areas, looking for a healthy getaway, frequent Club La Raquette on weekends.

Activities & Services

Aerobics, calisthenics, yoga, "Fitness with Finesse" (described above), "Survival of the Fittest" (a class for super athletes), stretching, massage, escorted 7 AM two-mile run, Lifecycles, treadmills, rowing machines, Stair Masters, Nautilus equipment and free weights, racquetball, squash, swimming, saunas, whirlpools, tanning beds, discounted beauty treatments at the nearby Christine Valmy salon, themed fitness walks.

Lodging

Guests stay in attractively decorated hotel rooms with limited-edition French lithographs. An elegant touch: Hotel guests are given toiletries designed by Hermes.

Cuisine

French-inspired low-calorie cuisine is served during the spa breakfast and lunch in Le Patio restaurant. These inspiring dishes do a lot to improve diet food's poor image (calorie counts are indicated on the menu): fricassee of mussels with endive and lime, veal with a citronette sauce, quiche with mushrooms, tarragon and chervil, lamb

■ AFFORDABLE SPAS

steamed in thyme with mint-scented vegetables and raspberry feuillete.

Le Parker Meridien
118 West 57th Street 212-245-5000
New York, NY 10019 800-543-4300

PAWLING HEALTH MANOR

Hyde Park, New York $$
Open: Year-round

This New York health retreat has such a good reputation for quick, healthy weight loss that it attracts well-known people one would expect to find at an expensive spa. Among Pawling's celebrity guests are Cecily Tyson, Jessica Tandy and Miles Davis. Ford fashion models wanting to shed a fast five pounds also frequent this retreat.

Joy Gross, the director of Pawling Health Manor, looks like a television talk show hostess. Bursting with good health and *joie de vivre*, she's a walking advertisement for what healthy living can do for your looks and energy level. The author of *Thin Again*, *Improved Fitness in 30 Days* and *The Vegetarian Child*, Gross based the spa program on a strict, closely supervised diet, combined with comprehensive nutritional educational classes and workshops.

Because of the physical strain of fasting, guests aren't encouraged to exercise strenuously. Yoga and swimming are about as active as anyone gets. Pawling doesn't even offer an aerobics class. Most guests spend a lot of time participating in educational classes covering such subjects as body cleansing and detoxification, vegetarianism, and why fad diets don't work. After a week at Pawling, many guests know more about nutrition than they thought possible.

Located in historic Hyde Park, where Franklin Delano Roosevelt, the Astors and Vanderbilts once lived, the manor is an imposing old Georgian mansion on a hill overlooking

NORTHEASTERN SPAS

the Hudson River. Despite the large building and its lovely surroundings, nothing about this health retreat is particularly luxurious. "Functional" describes it best.

Activities & Services

Yoga, meditation, workout room, swimming, sunbathing, individual diet and nutritional counseling, massage, facial, beauty and makeup tips, cooking demonstrations, lectures and workshops, fashion shows, films.

Lodging

Accommodations are simple and comfortable. The main house offers 16 rooms. Rooms are also available in a motel unit and the Annex.

Cuisine

Simple, low-calorie vegetarian dishes are served. Sample dishes are eggplant steak, pineapple froth (a beverage), broccoli casserole, pea soup, lentil stew, four-bean stuffed tomatoes, fruit sundae with ricotta cheese. There's no set calorie count.

Pawling Health Manor
Box 401
Hyde Park, NY 12538   914-889-4141

■ AFFORDABLE SPAS

TENNANAH LAKESHORE LODGE SPA AND RETREAT

Roscoe, New York

$ and $$
Open: Year-round

Located deep in the Catskill Mountains, Tennanah is quiet and unpretentious, a no-frills spa with simple accommodations and a relaxed atmosphere.

Owner Marie Trupia has been slowly renovating this lakeside spa, built around the turn of the century. Although there's still a lot of work to be done, all guest rooms and activity areas have been refurbished.

Located three hours northwest of New York City, Tennanah attracts working women from the Big Apple who need a peaceful environment in which to de-stress and relax at very affordable prices.

Relaxation appears to be more important to most guests than working out. The most popular spa offerings are the European beauty treatments, such as the fango wrap and the reflexology treatments.

The spa's fitness activities are based on the Carayas technique—deep-stretching movements and high-intensity, painless omnipotential weightlifting aerobic rhythms. These exercises claim to do everything imaginable: improve flexibility, circulation and muscular balance; decrease tension, pain and stiffness; help combat degenerative diseases; improve sleep; strengthen back, hip and stomach muscles; stabilize blood pressure. The list goes on.

Tennanah offers seven-night, four-night and two-night weekend packages that include three meals a day (or a supervised fasting program), accommodations, exercise classes, evening activities (e.g., lectures), a daily massage, unlimited use of all facilities and a choice of various beauty and skincare treatments.

Activities & Services

Deep-stretching movements, Carayas technique exercises, dynamic movements (for skeletal alignment), salt-water Jacuzzi, sauna, massage, reflexology, facials, fango and herbal wraps, salt-glow or loofah rub, manicures, pedicures, lectures, cooking classes, nature hikes, swimming, tennis, paddleboating, rowing.

Lodging

Four types of rooms are available. Guests who really want to cut down on costs can opt for the room with basin only and bath down the hall (total price for six nights including meals, classes and accommodations is about $500). The other rooms vary in price and size. However, the most expensive "Deluxe II" rooms don't offer that much more than the less costly "Standard" rooms.

Cuisine

A healthy, wholesome low-calorie diet is served (no set calorie count). Favorite dishes include stuffed fish, chicken Kiev, salad with a tasty low-calorie dressing (which guests rave about) and multigrain bread baked on the premises. A juice fasting program, supervised by a registered nurse, is also available.

Tennanah Lakeshore Lodge Spa and Retreat
R.D. 2 Box 71   607-498-4900
Roscoe, NY 12776   800-922-LAKE

PENNSYLVANIA

DEERFIELD MANOR

$

East Stroudsburg, Pennsylvania   Open: May to November

Owner Frieda Eisenkraft's warmth and humor bring guests back to Deerfield Manor over and over again. In fact, the spa boasts a high return rate. If guests are out of shape, overweight or intimidated by fitness, Eisenkraft puts them at ease. She creates a very congenial environment for the clientele, which is mostly women.

Located in an old, cheerful white frame house in East Stroudsburg, Pennsylvania, the spa epitomizes charm — from its numerous nooks and crannies (perfect for reading or quiet moments) to the healthy geraniums gracing the window boxes.

Guests can participate in as many or as few spa activities as they choose. Most guests stay fairly active and focus on weight loss. Some women are in good shape; others want to shed some pounds — and do.

Upon arrival, each guest is interviewed to determine a diet and fitness program. Follow-up interviews are conducted throughout the week in order to adjust the prescribed program.

Eisenkraft believes that all work and no play makes for bored guests. Therefore, she balances spa activities with antiquing, visits to the local flea markets, attending local theatrical performances and other excursions.

Activities & Services

Aerobics, body workouts, calisthenics, dyna-bands (big rubber bands with weights attached), aquacise, yoga, relaxation techniques, massage (reflexology, shiatsu), group support sessions, cooking demonstrations, health-related lectures by university professors, tennis, swimming, personalized fitness and dietary evaluation.

Lodging

Country-quaint describes the decor of the rooms in the main house — lots of white wicker and brass with floral bedspreads and curtains. Contemporary accommodations for two or more are available in the newer adjacent lodge.

NORTHEASTERN SPAS

Cuisine

600 to 700 calories a day (which is about as low as you can get before you start fasting). Every morning, guests choose their meals from a daily gourmet menu, keeping within their calorie limit. Dishes from the diet menu include homemade soup, baked fresh fish, steamed vegetables, chef's salad. Supervised water or juice fasting programs are available upon request.

Deerfield Manor
R.D. 1, Route 402
East Stroudsburg, PA 18301   717-223-0160

THE GLASS DOOR SPA

$$$

Natrona Heights, Pennsylvania   Open: Year-round

A 60-acre private estate in the rolling hills of western Pennsylvania is the home of The Glass Door Spa. Located 20 miles north of Pittsburgh, this spa serves as a peaceful retreat, where guests can be pampered, rejuvenated or just left alone in the solarium to catch up on some reading.

The Glass Door is owned and operated by Claire Van Sciver Edmonston and her husband, Dr. George Edmonston. Before opening The Glass Door, the couple visited spas of all prices throughout the U.S. to get ideas. They wanted to create a European, full-service spa in an area of the country where one didn't exist. Thus, The Glass Door opened in April 1987 in rural western Pennsylvania.

The Glass Door can accommodate up to 22 guests at a time in the Manor House or the newer Chateau, complete with theme rooms including the "Royal Orleans," "Hollywood Suite," "New York, New York" or the equestrian-style "Belmont."

AFFORDABLE SPAS

The emphasis at this spa isn't on rapid weight loss, but on relaxation and retreat from outside tensions. All activities (listed below) are voluntary. Stays range from two to 26 days. Some guests find the environment comfortable enough to begin a stop-smoking program. Others come to enjoy the walking trails, indoor wet area with skylights and "at-home" atmosphere.

The Glass Door periodically offers discounted rates, for example, seven nights for the price of five, or from ten to 30 percent off, depending on the length of stay.

The guest ratio of men to women is approximately 1:4. However, more couples are attending the "Royal Fantasy Weekends" for birthday or anniversary getaways.

Activities & Services

Water aerobics, swimming, Jacuzzi, sauna, solarium, aerobics, dance, stretch classes, physical evaluation, goal-setting, individualized exercise program, Airdyne bicycle, Lifecycle, rowing machine, five-station Universal, computerized treadmill, walking/jogging trails, cross-country skiing, biking, outdoor basketball, tennis, fashion shows, full-service beauty salon, massage, manicure, waxing, facials, skin analysis, theme weekends, nearby golf, trips to horse shows, Pittsburgh theater trips, limousine service.

Lodging

The Manor House and Chateau offer intimate, homey accommodations. Single, double and triple rooms are priced accordingly. Some baths offer sunken whirlpool tubs; all are elegantly decorated with matching linens. Fresh flowers grace each room.

Cuisine

900 to 1,200 calories per day are served in The Glass Door's three dining areas. Diners in the attached greenhouse room enjoy a spectacular view of the countryside.

NORTHEASTERN SPAS

The chef specially prepares meals for vegetarians and guests with food allergies. Meals are elegantly served on china and crystal. Sample menu items are chicken, veal and seafood dishes, low-calorie desserts and fresh vegetables from the spa's own vegetable garden. Alcohol is available during the weekend packages.

The Glass Door Spa
Sugar Loaf Hill
Natrona Heights, PA 15065   412-826-1422

THE HIMALAYAN INSTITUTE

$$

Honesdale, Pennsylvania   Open: Year-round

Founded in 1971 by Sri Swami Rama, The Himalayan Institute isn't a spa in the strictest sense of the word. However, it's similar in many ways to a holistic health retreat. Its programs combine the latest health information with the ancient principles of yoga to help individuals manage the myriad of problems in modern life.

All of the institute's programs focus on personal growth and development, in areas such as stress reduction, health, diet, nutrition and general well-being. Seminars change quarterly and are rescheduled at the same time each year. Some last a weekend; others last ten days.

The serene, monastic atmosphere of the Himalayan Institute and its general philosophy—deeply rooted in Eastern religion—attract people who are knowledgeable about relaxation, meditation and other elements of the institute's programs.

But that doesn't mean a novice would feel out of place. The staff is extraordinarily patient—one of the benefits, perhaps, of all that meditation and yoga.

A three-day weight loss seminar includes instruction

on how to handle the physiological and psychological aspects of weight loss; how to change habits, develop an exercise program and eat for optimal nourishment and satisfaction. Of the five instructors teaching that seminar, three have medical degrees, one has a doctorate and another has a master's. Those impressive credentials and levels of expertise are typical of the institute.

Another seminar, entitled "Breathing, Exercise and Holistic Health," combines aerobic exercise, yoga and breathing exercises that release untapped energy reserves. Guests are taught how to perform those exercises while walking, jogging and stretching. They also learn how to design their own holistic health exercise program.

The comprehensive ten-day "Holistic Health Training Program" covers nutrition, cooking, fasting, cleansing and purification techniques, proper breathing, relaxation, biofeedback, yoga, aerobic exercise and silence. Participants are given a reading list and advised to read up on holistic health before attending the seminar.

Once a Catholic seminary, the institute is located in the Pocono Mountains. Among the features of its 422-acre campus are an organic vegetable garden, orchard, apiary, greenhouse and numerous hiking trails.

Activities & Services

Activities depend upon the seminar. Numerous three- and ten-day seminars are offered (in addition to longer programs) at different times of year. The institute's catalog lists dates and descriptions. A sampling of seminars, in addition to the aforementioned, includes "Diet and Nutrition," "Transition to Vegetarianism," "Freedom from Stress," "Learning to Appreciate Yourself " and "Habits, Addictions and Self-Defeating Behaviors." Recreational facilities include tennis, volleyball, hiking, lake swimming, ice skating and cross-country skiing in the winter.

Lodging

Accommodations include pleasant single rooms, which are on a first-come, first-serve basis. All other rooms are double occupancy.

Cuisine

Vegetarian, of course. The produce is from the institute's organic gardens. Meals consist primarily of whole grains, vegetables and legumes. No diet plan is offered.

The Himalayan Institute
Rural Route 1, Box 400   717-253-5551
Honesdale, PA 18431   800-433-5472

VERMONT

GOLDEN EAGLE HEALTH SPA

Stowe, Vermont $$
                                      Open: Summer

If one spouse likes to exercise but the other prefers trout fishing, or vice versa, the Golden Eagle might be the perfect vacation setting. Its traditional mountain resort activities and comprehensive health and fitness package promise something for everyone.

The Golden Eagle is located in Stowe, Vermont, a picture-perfect New England town with white church steeples, country inns, birch-lined trails and fresh mountain pools. Although it's most famous for its ski resorts, Stowe also brims with summer fun: outdoor concerts, craft fairs, auctions, ballooning, gliding and more. It's a vacation spot for the person or family wanting to combine recreational sports, sight-seeing and spa activities.

In spite of Stowe's many distractions, most Golden Eagle guests are committed to getting or staying in shape.

AFFORDABLE SPAS

The programs are very personalized. Because classes rarely exceed six people, spa-goers are guaranteed a lot of personal attention.

Before guests arrive, the Golden Eagle staff begins to design a health program for each person. Guests complete a questionnaire that helps determine their spa goals. Questions and answers include "What are your personal goals? A.) Personal life transformation. B.) Toning the body. C.) Having fun. D.) Meeting new people. E.) Seeing Vermont. F.) All of the above."

Upon arrival, guests meet with the staff to discuss their program. Guests can request a program that keeps them busy all day or one that adheres to a more leisurely pace.

Classes and activities — ranging from goal-setting and dance aerobics to nutritional lectures and massage — are offered every day.

Most guests are between the ages of 30 and 60. The ratio of men to women is about 2:3. (Golden Eagle's health and fitness program only operates during the summer.)

Activities & Services

Weight training, aquacise, dance aerobics, fitness evaluation, nutritional counseling, stretching, goal-setting, jogging, swimming, whirlpool, sauna, massage, health-related lectures, bicycling, tennis, trout fishing, mountain hiking, horseback riding, golf, van tours of the area.

Lodging

Single and double rooms, suites, efficiencies and family-sized apartments are available in an older Colonial building or in a new Bavarian-style chalet.

Cuisine

1,200 to 1,500 calories a day. At the beginning of the week, guests choose what they want to eat from a pre-set menu. Popular dishes include veal marsala, vegetable fish roll and broiled scrod.

NORTHEASTERN SPAS

Golden Eagle Health Spa
P.O. Box 110
Route 108   802-253-4811
Stowe, VT 05672   800-626-1010

NEW LIFE SPA

$$$

Stratton Mountain, Vermont   Open: Year-round

New Life Spa is located in the Liftline Lodge, an Austrian-style chalet in a popular Vermont ski area. During the winter, many skiers take advantage of the spa's fitness and diet program, because it makes a noticeable difference in their skiing ability.

The fitness activities help limber up under- or overused muscles. The Pritikin-based diet gives people energy and a clear head.

After a day on the slopes, a massage at New Life Spa is a healthy way to unwind. And a facial helps relax and protect skin from the moisture-robbing effects of the cold, windy winter weather.

New Life also offers a comprehensive summer spa program, designed to improve cardiovascular fitness, endurance and muscle tone. Hiking in Green Mountain National Forest replaces skiing as the main outdoor activity at that time of year.

When each guest arrives, the staff designs an intensive exercise and diet program based on individual needs and goals. A wide range of exercise classes are offered daily. The well-informed staff is eager to work with guests and explain everything from the benefits of a particular exercise to the importance of body awareness.

People who are out of shape and/or more than 20 pounds overweight probably won't feel at home here. "This is not a fat farm," stresses Spa Director Jimmy LeSage. There

51

AFFORDABLE SPAS

are classes tailored to all levels of fitness, even though most guests are in pretty good shape.

The spa can handle a maximum of 25 guests at a time. As a result, everyone receives a lot of attention.

Activities & Services

Aerobics, aquacise, body awareness, body conditioning, body contour, weight resistance training and strengthening, yoga, health-related lectures and workshops such as the "New Life Guide to Healthy Eating," sauna, hot tub, massage, facials, manicures, walks, "Swim for Fitness," hiking, golf, racquetball, tennis, films.

Lodging

The Liftline Lodge features Austrian-style rustic rooms and private baths. The lobby is paneled in pine and features two large fireplaces.

Cuisine

800 to 1,000 calories a day. The food is based on the Pritikin diet, high in complex carbohydrates. Sample dishes include pita bread pizza, strawberries Romanoff and paprika chicken.

New Life Spa
Liftline Lodge
R.D. 1, Box 144
Stratton Mountain, VT 05155 802-297-2600

THE SPA AT STOWE

Stowe, Vermont

$$$
Open: Year-round

This spa offers a first-rate program in a quaint New England setting. Stowe, a popular year-round resort with excellent skiing, looks like a Currier and Ives print. The spa is housed in The Green Mountain Inn, a meticulously restored hostelry built in 1883 and listed on the National Register of Historic Places.

During the winter, the spa successfully integrates skiing with its overall program. Guests are provided with quality ski equipment so they don't have to buy or rent their own. The spa/ski instructors teach guests how to ski if they're new to the sport and help experienced skiers improve their skills.

Guests can cross-country ski along the groomed trails of the Trapp Family Lodge or opt for downhill skiing at Mount Mansfield.

The Spa at Stowe has plenty besides skiing to offer: Nautilus training circuit, steam bath, sauna, exercise classes, one-on-one instruction and more.

Included in the spa package is a musculoskeletal evaluation and fitness screening test to determine percentage of body fat and overall health risk. The test is supervised by an exercise physiologist and physical therapist. An exercise prescription and nutritional plan are offered to each guest based on his/her test results and lifestyle.

One unique feature is the week-long "Fit Kids" program, which attracts a lot of mothers and children. "We have a nutritionist who talks to the kids," says the spa owner and director, Gene Meehan. "But it only lasts about as long as it takes to eat a peanut butter and jelly sandwich. You can't very well lecture a kid. A dentist teaches them about tooth care, plus there's lots of physical activity. The kids are taken care of all day so their parents can do other things."

The program is offered the first week of each month during the summer. Parents interested in the program

AFFORDABLE SPAS

should make reservations well in advance. Only ten children are accepted per week.

About half the spa guests are women. More and more men are participating in the spa programs each year. However, usually they're "dragged in here kicking and screaming by girlfriends or wives," says Meehan. "But they all seem to like the program once they get into it."

The program accommodates 25 to 30 guests at a time, ensuring lots of personal attention.

In addition to its many outdoor attractions, Stowe is full of quaint shops and restaurants. A wide range of activities takes place throughout the year, such as Mozart concerts, antique auctions, dog shows and summer theater.

Activities & Services

Low-impact aerobics, aerobic stretch, aquacise, stretch and flex (flexercise), hiking, walks, jogging, yoga, steam bath, sauna, whirlpool, tanning room, massage, facials, Nautilus training circuit, Lifecycles, bicycling, nutritional counseling, fitness testing, skiing, ice skating, polo, windsurfing, swimming, cooking demonstrations, lectures and seminars on health or skiing, personal fitness profile.

Lodging

The Inn's attractively decorated guest rooms are furnished with Early American reproduction furniture. Some rooms have four-poster canopy beds.

Cuisine

Low-calorie food is served in the Inn's main dining room and the Whip Lounge. A calorie count is listed next to each item. Guests are encouraged not to exceed 1,200 calories a day, if they're interested in losing weight. Dishes include crepe Florentine with greens and herb dressing, cold poached salmon with cucumber dill sauce, veal loin chop and grilled fresh Idaho trout with lime.

NORTHEASTERN SPAS

The Spa at Stowe
Green Mountain Inn
P.O. Box 1198
Stowe, VT 05672

802-253-9954
800-525-5606

CHAPTER 3

Southern Spas and Fitness Resorts

3

FLORIDA

THE FONTAINEBLEU HILTON RESORT AND SPA

Miami Beach, Florida

$$$/Summer
Open: Year-round

Located along Miami's oceanfront, The Fontainebleu is one busy place — 1,200 rooms with a 75 percent year-round occupancy rate. This luxurious spa and resort boasts every service imaginable, numerous restaurants, bars, entertainment centers and shops. It also features a half-acre free-form swimming pool with a cascading waterfall and a juice bar beneath a rock grotto.

The high-rise resort spa attracts an equal number of men and women. (The fact that The Fontainebleu is one of the largest convention hotels in the U.S. accounts for the number of men.) The spa is popular with families, young and old. Young families take advantage of the children's programs. And many adults bring their parents.

"We have low-impact aerobics, morning beach walks and reach and stretch for the parents," explains spa

AFFORDABLE SPAS

Secretary/Treasurer John Horvitz. "Then regular and more strenuous aerobics for the 'aerobic animals.'"

Upon arrival, guests are given an individual guided tour of the facilities. They complete a questionnaire and are tested for body fat and fitness levels. That information is analyzed by a computer, and a counselor helps determine appropriate exercises and a maintenance program.

The spa offers a wide range of exercise classes (14 daily), beauty and relaxation treatments, personal instruction and lectures. Especially popular are the beauty treatments in the Christine Valmy salon, a wonderful place to overindulge in numerous exotic beauty services (e.g., ultra-live cell and byogenic treatments — those go on your face).

The salon is the Bloomingdale's of beauty remedies and treatments (most of which are a la carte). It also features special packages: "The Beachgoer," which includes eyelash tint, full leg and bikini wax, underarm wax and pedicure; and "After Beach," which includes full body moisturizing, instant face revitalizer, and hand and foot nail touch-up.

From May 1 to December 15, this luxurious spa and resort meets *Affordable Spas and Fitness Resorts* pricing standards for a $$$ spa. Although prices are higher during the winter, the Fontainebleu features special weekend spa packages throughout the year.

Activities & Services

Beginning, intermediate and advanced aerobics, morning beach walks, total conditioning, body sculpturing, aquacise, reach and stretch, ballet stretch, evening walks, gym with free weights and Nautilus equipment, computerized fitness evaluation, whirlpool, sauna, steam room, Jacuzzi, solarium, swimming, tennis, boating. The Christine Valmy Salon offers so many beauty treatments we can list only a sampling: skincare treatments for everyone from executives to teenagers, massage, makeup lessons, makeovers, herbal wraps, manicures and pedicures.

SOUTHERN SPAS

Lodging

Many rooms have sweeping ocean views. They are nicely decorated and stocked with such amenities as shampoos and body lotion.

Cuisine

Two low-calorie spa meals are offered daily in most of the resort's seven restaurants. A calorie count for each item is indicated on the menu. Sample dishes are broccoli, cauliflower and artichokes with garlic sauce, chilled gazpacho, lobster bisque and grilled Florida pompano (a local seafood specialty). The Veranda restaurant in the spa serves fresh natural foods, such as imaginative salads, sandwiches, fresh juices, fruit smoothies and natural desserts. Granny Feelgoods serves health food.

The Fontainebleu Hilton Resort and Spa
4441 Collins Avenue   305-538-2000
Miami Beach, FL 33140   800-HILTONS

HARBOR ISLAND SPA

North Bay Village, Florida $$
                                      Open: Year-round

This modern Florida spa is located on a private island in Biscayne Bay, only a few minutes from Miami. Most of its patrons are women over 50 who want to lose weight. However, that's starting to change as more men and people in their thirties check in to the spa.

Harbor Island Spa's weight loss/fitness program is comprehensive and professionally executed. Before arriving, guests complete a chart that indicates height, weight, measurements of the chest, waist, hip and thigh, pulse rate and blood pressure.

AFFORDABLE SPAS

That information enables the dietician to prescribe a diet, which guests can also follow at home. It also helps the fitness director design an appropriate exercise regimen. The staff physician, who conducts a medical review of each new guest, also uses the information provided on the chart.

Spa activities range from aerobics, yoga and slimnastics to massage and body wrap. Guests can participate in as many activities as they like or do nothing more strenuous than improve their tan.

Resort and extracurricular activities include everything from tennis clinics and golf to shopping excursions and visits to the nearby race track.

While nightly entertainment at most spas usually means a lecture on nutrition, Harbor Island swings with live entertainment and dinner dancing to the spa orchestra.

Be sure to inquire about the numerous attractive packages for three-, four- and seven-night stays.

Activities & Services

Aerobics, slimnastics, yoga, aquacise, posture analysis, nutritional counseling and lectures, weight loss rap sessions, massage, facial, body wraps, herbal wraps, makeup lessons, dance classes, loofah salt rubs, sauna, whirlpool, steam room, tennis, swimming in a mineral salt water Olympic-size pool and exercise pool, fully equipped gym.

Lodging

Single or double rooms are available in the economically priced Spa Building. The more expensive Bayfront Tower Suites and Pool Lanai Suites boast views.

Cuisine

Daily calorie consumption varies with the individual and type of diet. Each day, guests choose what they want to eat from a special menu. For dinner, guests might have a choice between roast prime rib of kosher beef, grilled spring chicken, broiled fillet of rainbow trout or broiled lamb patties.

Harbor Island Spa
7900 Larry Paskow Way   305-751-7561
North Bay Village, FL 33141   800-772-7546 (out of state)

LIDO SPA HOTEL

$

Miami Beach, Florida   Open: Year-round

This Florida spa is a bargain-hunter's dream come true. During the busy winter season, a six-night stay (including accommodations, all meals and spa activities) costs approximately $500. Price-wise, it can't get much better. However, don't expect luxurious amenities and trendy decorating. The Lido is a standard motel located on Biscayne Bay in the heart of Miami Beach.

Most guests take advantage of surrounding attractions and activities, such as Lincoln Road Mall, the Omni Plaza, jai alai, dog races, Bayside Market Place, the art deco district, Bal Harbor shopping and more.

The Lido attracts middle-aged men and women and senior citizens. Half the guests want to lose weight; the other half want to have fun and relax. Guests at the Lido Spa Hotel dance the night away. The hotel features a regular night club act with live music.

For those who are in good shape (and under 45), the Lido probably won't be very challenging. However, for older men and women interested in starting a diet/exercise program or reviving one that has lapsed, the Lido is ideal.

The exercise classes aren't at all intimidating, regardless of a guest's physical condition. Upon arrival, guests meet with the dietician and spa director to develop a program to fit their personal needs and goals. Guests who

AFFORDABLE SPAS

plan to participate in fitness activities receive a medical check-up.

Activities & Services

Aerobics, yoga, aquacise, exercise equipment, loofah rub, massage, diagnostic laboratory and medical examination facilities, nutritional counseling, guest speakers, steam rooms and cabinets, saunas, eight individual whirlpools, mineral bath, three swimming pools, walks, concerts, nightclub acts, live music, movies.

Lodging

Guests stay in a two-floor standard motel. Also available are apartments with kitchens, where guests can create their own low-calorie meals.

Cuisine

Diet and nondiet food is served; calorie count depends on individual needs and goals. Low-calorie dishes prepared without salt or sugar include eggplant Parmesan, vegetable loaf, strawberry fluff and spa chicken. Nondiet food includes veal chop, lobster Lido and red snapper.

Lido Spa Hotel
40 Belle Island
Venetian Causeway
Miami Beach, FL 33139

303-538-4621
800-327-8363 (out of state)
800-824-2746 (Canada)

WEIGHT WATCHERS AT NEWPORT PIER HOLIDAY INN

Miami Beach, Florida

$$

Open: Year-round

Anyone who's serious about weight loss will be in good hands at the Weight Watchers' program at Newport Pier Holiday Inn. This beachfront hotel, which recently underwent a $30 million dollar face-lift, boasts a penthouse-level fitness center and pool.

The program is based on Weight Watchers' diet plan, daily exercise and motivational classes and workshops. The staff helps each guest develop a personalized exercise plan that suits one's lifestyle and diet goals. (Spa-goers can continue the program at home, with the added benefit of attending local Weight Watchers' meetings.)

The staff is very supportive and sensitive to guests' concerns. Most Weight Watchers' teachers were once overweight themselves.

Guests are encouraged to participate in the exercise classes. However, all activities are optional. Guests can lounge around the pool, do aerobics from morning to night or go sight-seeing.

Learning a new and better way to eat is the ultimate goal of the Weight Watchers' program. Behavioral change and ongoing reinforcement are the backbone of the program. Guests learn how to plan menus and prepare food the Weight Watchers' way, how to take charge when dining out and how to manage stress, sustain motivation and increase self-esteem.

A typical day's offerings might include a morning stretch class, a stretch and tone (flexercise) class, aerobics, water exercises and a walk. Among the afternoon activities are a workshop or lecture, race walking and yoga.

Like spas elsewhere, Weight Watchers offers a wide range of beauty treatments — everything from massage to body wraps.

■ AFFORDABLE SPAS

Activities & Services

Aerobics, aquacise, stretch and tone, yoga, walks, lectures and behavior modification workshops, personal exercise program, nutritional counseling, group support sessions, massage, facials, herbal body wraps, loofah body polish, hand and foot massage, manicure, pedicure, makeup application lessons, swimming. Nearby golf, tennis and fishing.

Lodging

Some rooms have ocean views, others have bay views. Rooms facing east and south have balconies from which guests can enjoy sunrises and cool ocean breezes.

Cuisine

1,000 to 1,200 calories a day. Sample dishes are red snapper with sesame vegetables, linguine with bay scallops and honeyed pumpkin custard.

Weight Watchers at Newport Pier Holiday Inn
16701 Collins Avenue
Miami Beach, FL 33160

For more information on the Newport Pier Holiday Inn program and the Weight Watchers spa programs at other locations, contact

Weight Watchers Resorts and Spas	313-443-1414
15815 W. 12 Mile Road	800-LEANER-U
Southfield, MI 48076	800-826-5088 (Canada)

SOUTHERN SPAS

THE SPA AT PALM-AIRE

Pompano Beach, Florida

$$$/Summer
Open: Year-round

The Spa at Palm-Aire is one of the most written about and photographed spas in the world. (Robin Leach of "Lifestyles of the Rich and Famous" called it "one of the world's best spas.") It attracts a wide range of guests—from homemakers to ambassadors. The elegant spa's most impressive endorsement has come from Elizabeth Taylor, who publicly thanked the spa for slimming her down to a size 6.

For most of the year, the Palm-Aire would be off limits to anyone seeking an affordable spa escape. But during the summer, it offers reasonably priced day, weekend and week-long packages. More and more super spas such as this one are offering discounts to keep their off-season lively. (At the time of this writing, The Spa at Palm-Aire also offered summer guests and a friend 60 percent discounts on Eastern Airlines coach fares or 30 percent off first class.)

Fitness, stress reduction and beauty treatments are offered to all guests—who run the gamut from celebrities to executives to homemakers wanting to shed five to ten pounds. Upon arrival, all guests consult with the resident physician. Spa programs are tailored to each person's needs. Among the spa's fitness specialties is an imaginative assortment of water exercise classes.

Men's and women's spa facilities are separate. Coed facilities include the racquetball court, 25-yard pool, sundeck, parcourse and gym (with $100,000 worth of new exercise equipment).

Last summer, the spa underwent an extensive refurbishment. Now the women's spa resembles a lovely garden room, decorated in shades of green, peach and white with chintz upholstery and wall coverings, wicker furniture, columns with trellises, and lush tropical plants. The men's spa, decorated in blue and beige with lots of wood, has a very clubby feeling.

AFFORDABLE SPAS

The spa recently added a number of wonderful new beauty treatments to the program, including a good-enough-to-eat moisturizing whirlpool bath—scented with orange blossom, peach, strawberry, apricot, musk, cocoa butter and foaming milk.

The 1,500-acre Palm-Aire resort, a luxury development in Pompano Beach, includes the hotel and spa, condominiums, a conference center, golf course, tennis courts and other sports facilities, and the new University Health Center (a state-of-the-art wellness program that exceeds the price range used for this book).

Activities & Services

Aquacise and other swimming exercises (including a paddle class and aqua gym float class), whirlpools, saunas, steam rooms, gym with Body Master equipment, sundeck, parcourse, indoor racquetball courts, tennis, golf, massage, facials, salt glow loofah scrub, full body herbal wrap, hot paraffin facial mask, cold paraffin body cream treatment, body composition analysis, manicure, pedicure, full-service beauty salon, lectures on behavior modification, stress management, nutrition and other health-related topics.

Lodging

Guests stay in spacious rooms with private terraces and dressing rooms. Toiletries are provided.

Cuisine

Palm-Aire has a special Spa Dining Room that serves an 800-calorie diet to women and 1,000-calorie diet to men. The food is so superb, it hardly seems like a diet. Sample dishes include fettucini with seafood marinara, tenderloin kabob over rice and coconut pineapple cheesecake (40 calories per serving).

SOUTHERN SPAS

The Spa at Palm-Aire
2551 Palm-Aire Drive North
Pompano Beach, FL 33069

305-975-6122
800-327-4960

REGENCY HEALTH RESORT AND SPA

$$

Hallandale, Florida   **Open: Year-round**

This well-rounded spa is located on a pristine beach 15 minutes from Fort Lauderdale in South Florida's Gold Coast. The spa's programs are rooted in holistic health. However, unlike most holistic spas, everything about Regency—from the way it looks to the clientele—is very mainstream. For the uninitiated, it's a good place to be introduced to holistic health.

Dr. Gregory Haag, a physician and holistic health advocate, creates a personalized health and diet program for any interested guest. The programs are designed to help guests learn how to eat properly for weight loss or maintenance. Guests also learn how their health is affected by emotional, mental and physical factors.

Every day, each guest's blood pressure, weight and pulse rate are monitored. The daily schedule of voluntary activities includes everything from walks on the beach, stretch and tone (flexercise) and aerobics to meditation and behavior modification seminars—designed to help guests make permanent lifestyle changes.

The spa's educational programs give guests a well-balanced selection, integrating the types of classes offered at holistic spas, beauty-oriented spas, athletic spas and weight loss spas.

About 80 percent of Regency's guests are women, many of whom are career-oriented. Athletic spa-goers would probably find the spa too easy.

AFFORDABLE SPAS

Activities & Services

Yoga, stretch-er-cize, guided relaxation, aerobics, touch and tone, aquacise, gym, walks, nutritional counseling, stress management, behavior modification, health-related lectures and workshops, facials, massage, manicure, pedicure, full-service beauty salon, food preparation classes, Jacuzzi, sauna, swimming.

Lodging

Acommodations are standard Florida hotel rooms — light, airy rooms, accented in pastel colors with bamboo furniture. Ocean-view luxury apartments are also available.

Cuisine

The vegetarian diet consists of organic fruit, vegetables, nuts, seeds and whole grains. Guests are encouraged to eat as much food as they want. The food at the Regency is so low in calories that even serious dieters can overindulge and still lose weight. Supervised juice and water fasting programs are available.

Regency Health Resort and Spa
2000 S. Ocean Drive
Hallandale, FL 33009   305-454-2220

RUSSELL HOUSE

Key West, Florida

$, $$ and $$$
Open: Year-round

At Russell House, the emphasis is on how to improve your life through behavior modification, education and positive thinking.

SOUTHERN SPAS

If guests want to lose weight, stop smoking or kick other negative habits, this spa provides a comfortable place to do it.

The atmosphere at Russell House is so casual that guests can dine in a wet bathing suit, if they're so inclined. About half of the daily activities are fitness-related. The remaining programs are educational, such as lectures on disease prevention and lifestyle changes for healthier living. Numerous stress management workshops are offered.

Guests choose which classes they want to attend; there is no pressure to do everything. A guest can be very busy one day and choose to relax by the pool the next day.

Private consultations with the staff about health, fitness, nutrition, dieting and personal well-being are encouraged. However, in keeping with the relaxed atmosphere, it's up to the guest to initiate these discussions. The staff is very accessible and informative.

The mostly female clientele at Russell House comes from all over the country. Increasing numbers of westerners are checking into the spa.

Guests who've never visited Key West before are in for a treat. For years, this quaint historic town has been a haven for artists and writers. (Ernest Hemingway once lived here.) The Victorian architecture and tropical landscape add to its charm. Shops and art galleries line charming Duval Street.

Every evening at dusk, people gather at Mallory Pier to celebrate Key West's spectacular sunsets and enjoy local entertainment. Russell House guests are encouraged to join in this nightly tradition at least once, as well as take advantage of Key West's other attractions: sailing, snorkeling and walks along the beach.

Activities & Services

Yoga, breathing exercises, stretching, aquacise, flexercise, gentle movement, walks, swimming, massage (dry brush, Swedish, deep tissue, reflexology, acupressure and shiatsu), European beauty wraps, herbal wraps, paraffin

AFFORDABLE SPAS

wraps, cellulite treatments, full-body herbal steam treatments, manicure, pedicure, full-service beauty salon. Seminars and workshops on subjects such as stress reduction, behavior modification, nutrition, heart disease, cancer, arthritis, holistic health, lifestyle change, smoking elimination, creative visualization, relaxation techniques, mind control. Acupuncture, chiropractic medicine, astrology.

Lodging

Single, double, triple and dormitory accommodations are available and priced accordingly. The rooms are simple and unpretentious.

Cuisine

The vegetarian menu includes calorie counts for each item. Guests choose what they want to eat, within their suggested calorie limit. A 550-calorie diet is recommended for those who are serious about knocking off some pounds. (Guests on this diet have been known to lose up to ten pounds a week.) Juice fasting is also available. Sample menu items are vegetable stir-fry and brown noodle spaghetti.

Russell House
611 Truman Avenue
Key West, FL 33040   305-294-8787

SAFETY HARBOR SPA AND FITNESS CENTER

Safety Harbor, Florida

$$$/Summer
Open: Year-round

Located on the west shore of old Tampa Bay, Safety Harbor is the oldest and largest continuously operated spa in the U.S. It is fed by five mineral springs, discovered in the

16th century by Hernando DeSoto.

In 1926, a pavilion with high domed ceilings and massive beams was built over the main spring. Today, the pavilion serves as the spa's dining room. The Mediterranean architecture, moss-covered oak trees, herons and pelicans create a relaxing atmosphere.

The spa offers a multitude of daily exercise classes plus evening lectures and outings to discount clothing stores such as Loehmann's. The instructors are professional and well-informed.

Until recently, this spa was off-limits year-round to anyone seeking an affordable spa escape. However, in 1986 Safety Harbor started offering special spa packages that meet the pricing standards of this book (approximately $1,000 for seven nights, double occupancy accommodations, all meals, exercise classes and facilities). During the rest of the year prices are higher.

Although the off-season in Florida tends to be hot, spa-goers are indoors most of the time. And the spa is less crowded, so guests receive more personal attention.

The spa also offers a "Beautiful Day" program — eight hours of head-to-toe treatments in the spa's Lancome Institut de Beaute. It includes hairstyling, makeup application lessons and applications, eyebrow shaping, facials, manicures, pedicures, a vast assortment of haircare and skincare therapies and more.

Most of Safety Harbor's guests are women over 40. Dinner at this spa is more formal than at many others. Fashions include everything from the latest couture resortwear to rhinestone-studded warm-up suits.

Activities & Services

Low-impact aerobics, aquacise, stretching, body definition, circuit weight training, calisthenics, rubber band resistance, back classes, free weights, triathlon, nutritional counseling, fitness profile, massage, facials, loofah salt glow, herbal wrap, manicure, pedicure, full-service Lancome salon, lectures on subjects such as behavior modification, cooking demonstrations, whirlpool, sauna, solarium, therapy pool filled with mineral water, walks, swimming, tennis, golf, bicycling, dancing and casino entertainment.

Lodging

Guests stay in large rooms with dressing areas, balconies and bay views. Lancome amenities are provided. Spa waters are brought to rooms upon request.

Cuisine

900 to 1,200 calories a day are served. Nondieters are served full fare (larger portions of the spa food). Sample items from the menu are gazpacho, bouillabaisse, Bayou snapper Creole, pasta shells stuffed with crabmeat, bananas baked with lime. Although a lounge at Safety Harbor serves alcohol, it isn't recommended for guests wanting to lose weight. Another lounge offers a "Drink to Your Health Campaign" with free tastings of nonalcoholic red and white wines, fitness cocktails (e.g., nonalcoholic daiquiris) and mineral waters from all over the world. A juice bar is available twice a day.

Safety Harbor Spa and Fitness Center
105 N. Bayshore Drive
Safety Harbor, FL 34695

813-726-1161
800-237-0155

SONESTA SANIBEL HARBOUR RESORT

Fort Myers, Florida

$$$/Summer
Open: Year-round

Sonesta Sanibel is a resort that thinks big. It has a 40,000-square-foot spa and fitness center and the Jimmy Conners U.S. Tennis Center (he's part owner of the resort). Dramatic in appearance, the high-tech spa is located under

SOUTHERN SPAS

the resort's 5,000-seat stadium. Appointed in gold inlay, its ceiling, which resembles a staircase, is a sight to behold.

The spa program includes daily exercise classes, beauty and relaxation therapies (such as loofah scrubs, herbal wraps and massage). Upon request, a fitness instructor and nutritionist can design a personalized diet and exercise program. However, most guests are on vacation and not overly concerned with serious spa activities. The atmosphere is relaxed and fun, not competitive.

The spa has state-of-the-art computerized Keiser workout equipment. It also has separate exercise rooms for men and women and a coed workout area.

The tennis program at Sonesta is the best. It features 13 lighted clay and composition courts, a world-class stadium that hosts many first-rate matches, a teaching pro staff, video teaching aids and instructional programs.

Fort Myers is a Florida paradise: a charming, Gulf Coast town full of tropical beauty and ringed with white sand beaches. The Caloosahatchee River divides old town Fort Myers from the newer neighborhoods. The local beaches are noted for their shells and sand castle contests.

Most of the year, Sonesta Sanibel's prices are in excess of this book's maximum rate. However, during the summer the resort lowers its prices, giving spa-goers an opportunity to experience a first-rate resort at affordable prices.

Athletes and professionals make up the majority of spa-goers. Sonesta is also a good vacation spot for singles and families.

Activities & Services

Aerobics, aquacise, Keiser equipment, weight training room, saunas, steam rooms, whirlpools, swimming, racquetball, Swiss showers, massage, facials, herbal wraps, loofah scrubs, tennis. Nearby areas of interest: Sanibel Island, Captiva Island and Fort Myers Beach.

■ AFFORDABLE SPAS

Lodging

One-, two- and three-bedroom apartments, tastefully decorated in soft peach and light natural colors, are available. Some have kitchens and balconies overlooking San Carlos Bay and Sanibel Island.

Cuisine

Sonesta's Jimmy Conners Restaurant and the Matchpoint Pub offer guests gourmet or casual dining. However, neither restaurant offers low-calorie cuisine. Guests also enjoy Fort Myers' seafood restaurants and shrimp houses.

Sonesta Sanibel Harbour Resort
17260 Harbour Point Drive   813-466-4000
Fort Myers, FL 33908   800-343-7170

KENTUCKY

BLUEGRASS SPA

Stamping Ground, Kentucky

$$ and $$$
Open: Late April to Early November

Nestled in idyllic Kentucky countryside, Bluegrass Spa promises variety—everything from creative fitness activities to metaphysical programs. Guests can participate in physical conditioning programs, take advantage of the beauty treatments (including nonsurgical face-lifts) or attend lectures on such subjects as guided imagery, expanded consciousness and meditation.

Aside from the diversity of programs and services, Bluegrass Spa is also noteworthy for its lovely scenery. Famous for its horse-breeding farms, Stamping Ground is the picture-perfect country often featured on television

SOUTHERN SPAS

during Kentucky Derby season. While walking along the quiet country roads near the spa, guests can see beautiful old tobacco barns and some of the country's most elegant horse farms. Even the stone and wood fences around the farms are works of art.

Housed in a Greek revival antebellum mansion (circa 1813), the spa is surrounded by seven guest houses and rolling Kentucky bluegrass lawns and fields. From the quilts on the beds to the nouvelle diet cuisine, Bluegrass Spa blends country charm and graciousness with sophistication. Southern hospitality reigns supreme.

The spa attracts many career women who want to develop a healthier, less stressful lifestyle or who are interested in learning about holistic health. The age range of guests is typically between 30 and 60.

Attendance for the exercise classes is voluntary; however, the majority of guests participates in most of the daily activities listed below. After the first few days, guests start encouraging each other to keep up the good work, whether it's losing weight, toning muscles or relaxing.

Because the spa can accommodate only 12 guests at a time, patrons are guaranteed plenty of personal attention, pampering and privacy.

Activities & Services

Low-impact aerobics, yoga, body movement, mini-trampoline, aquacise, slow stretch and relaxation, body awareness, creative movement, T'ai Chi. Swedish, Trager, shiatsu, polarity and reflexology massage. Aromatherapy facial, deep cleansing facial, rejuvenating scalp treatment, hand and foot wax therapy, makeup and color analysis, nonsurgical face-lift. Lectures and workshops on subjects such as stress, astrology, preventive health care, how to read food labels, exercise myths. Bicycling, walks, swimming, tennis, golf, horseback riding, croquet, field trips to Kentucky Horse Park (Man-O-War has a shrine here), Shakertown at Pleasant Hill, antique shopping on Railroad Street, Phoenix Institute.

■ AFFORDABLE SPAS

Lodging

Guest rooms in the main house feature fireplaces and porches. (Because these rooms are so popular, reservations should be made well in advance.) The cabanas and lodge rooms, appointed in wicker and antiques, are located next to the pool. Accommodations are available for singles, doubles and three or more.

Cuisine

900 calories a day. Spa-goers eat a modified Pritikin diet without fats, salts or sugar. The nouvelle cuisine menu includes dishes such as garden vegetable tortilla with salsa, chilled peach glow soup, baked lime snapper with papaya chutney, chicken with 40 cloves of garlic, chocolate mousse. Frozen grapes and bananas are available throughout the day for snacking.

Bluegrass Spa
901 Galloway Road
Stamping Ground, KY 40379   502-535-6261

LOUISIANA

AVENUE PLAZA HOTEL/EUROVITA SPA
$$$
New Orleans, Louisiana   Open: Year-round

The Avenue Plaza Hotel sits in the heart of New Orleans' Garden District. The elegant stone building, constructed in the 1940s, has all the southern charm of St. Charles Avenue, with its wide street and trolley cars.

In 1986, the Avenue Plaza converted its expansive first floor to a spa and exercise facility. The staff, under the direction of Dr. Christopher Breuleux, created a continental atmosphere and called it "EuroVita" — Euro for the European feel and Vita for living to the fullest.

Beautifully decorated in peach, mauve and dusty green, the spa boasts state-of-the-art exercise equipment and luxurious locker areas, in which guests are provided with towels, robes, hair dryers, toiletries and oak lockers. Also provided is the spa's own line of beauty products called EuroVITA.

Classes are offered throughout the day. However, most guests prefer working out in the equipment room, which includes a cardiovascular area and a strength area. A physician is available to give health-risk appraisals and computerized fitness analysis/prescription.

Guests also can take in lectures by nutritionists, cosmetic surgeons, registered dieticians and physicians, or attend a class in the aerobics/dance studio, which has a shock-absorbing Exerflex floor. A rooftop Jacuzzi and juice bar offer a spectacular skyline view of New Orleans, the Superdome and the Mississippi River.

The ratio of men to women is 2:3. The peak season for the Avenue Plaza is, of course, during Mardi Gras. However, attractive packages are offered throughout the year, including a half-day stress reliever, a day of beauty, a two-night spa sampler or a three- or six-night fitness package.

Activities & Services

Aerobics, yoga, body toning, stretch exercises, video exercise room for private workouts, Scandinavian saunas, Turkish steam baths, Swiss showers, individual whirlpools, rooftop Jacuzzi, courtyard swimming pool, tanning solarium, herbal wraps, loofah salt glow rub, Swedish and shiatsu massage, unisex beauty salon, facials, makeup, manicures, pedicures, waxing, color analysis, Universal and Paramount resistance machines, free weights, exercise bicycles, treadmill, Stair Master, Versa Climber and acumassage table (an electonically powered massage table).

■ AFFORDABLE SPAS

Lodging

Guests at Avenue Plaza Hotel stay in suites with enclosed kitchen units and wet bars. Separate living rooms are available. Guests can choose traditional decor or art deco rooms decorated in deep maroon, gray and black.

Cuisine

There's no set calorie limit at the Avenue Plaza. Low-calorie breakfast and lunch are served in the spa cafe, and juice and mineral water are served throughout the day. The hotel doesn't offer an evening meal because the staff believes that guests should taste the flavors of New Orleans by sampling dishes in its famous restaurants. This makes the daily workouts all the more important.

Avenue Plaza Hotel/EuroVita Spa
2111 Saint Charles Avenue   504-566-1212
New Orleans, LA 70130   800-535-9575

TEXAS

FOUR SEASONS HOTEL AND RESORT
$$$
Irving, Texas   **Open: Year-round**

The Four Seasons is a best bet for anyone who enjoys shaping up in a luxurious environment. The beautiful resort near Dallas combines the amenities of a first-rate hotel with a comprehensive spa program. The latter features fitness activities, beauty and pampering services and imaginative low-calorie cuisine.

The Four Seasons is very popular with professionals, many of whom combine a business trip with spa activities. Most guests (about 70 percent) are men.

SOUTHERN SPAS

Spa-goers at the Four Seasons are more concerned with fitness than dieting. Before arriving, guests receive a form asking such questions as "What are your fitness and diet goals?" "Do you like an unstructured itinerary or a more regimented one?" "What times of the day do you prefer to exercise?" "Do you want one-on-one help or do you prefer to work on your own?"

Guests mail questionnaires back to the spa before the date of their arrival. The staff—made up of sports, fitness, health and nutrition professionals—then uses that information to design a personalized program.

Hotel guests can use the spa for the day or the weekend, or can sign up for four- or seven-day spa packages. The packages include a "Health and Lifestyle Profile" (a ten- to 15-page computerized analysis of an individual's nutritional and dietary needs and risk factors such as heart disease). The spa staff interprets the results and can counsel guests accordingly.

No one at the Four Seasons lives in sweats night and day. Nightlife can be an elegant occasion. Dinner at the Four Seasons gives people a chance to call it a day at the spa and dress to the nines.

The resort and spa are elegantly appointed in the very latest in colors, furnishings and architectural details. The spa, decorated with beautiful tile, is furnished in comfortable contemporary wicker. A spectacular indoor cushioned jogging track encircles the top of the exercise room.

Located at Las Colinas, a beautifully landscaped office park and community surrounded by rolling hills, the 400-acre Four Seasons also offers traditional resort activities, listed below.

Activities & Services

Aerobics, aquacise, sports stretch, weight training, dance, karate, facials. Swedish, shiatsu and aromatherapy massage. Aromatherapy baths, herbal wraps and baths, loofah-salt scrub, tanning beds, manicure, pedicure, full-

AFFORDABLE SPAS

service beauty salon. Nutritional, dietary and fitness classes and counseling. Saunas, cold plunges, steam rooms, whirlpools, swimming, tennis, racquetball, golf.

Lodging

Rooms in the first-rate Four Seasons Hotel are beautifully decorated. Among the amenities one finds are thick terry robes and hair dryers.

Cuisine

A 1,000-calories-a-day diet is served in the Cafe on the Green. Nondiet food is also available there. Included on the Four Seasons menu are such dishes as pasta primavera and curry chicken salad.

Four Seasons Hotel and Resort
4150 North MacArthur Boulevard
Irving, TX 75038   214-717-0700

GUADALUPE RIVER RANCH AND HEALTH ENHANCEMENT CENTER

Boerne, Texas $$$/Weekends
                                     Open: Year-round

The magnificent Guadalupe River Ranch is perched on a bluff overlooking the river for which it's named. Built in the 1920s, the rustic stone buildings and walkways, verandas, grottos and gazebos blend with the majestic oak trees to create a tranquil atmosphere.

In the late seventies, Broadway producer Walter Starcke bought the 380-acre ranch and turned it into a holistic health retreat. He continually updates the facilities, all the while maintaining the original ranch architecture.

The backdrop for the Guadalupe River Ranch is a breathtakingly beautiful landscape. Says Ranch Director

Mike Ezzell, "This is a very special healing environment. There's an indescribable feeling at Guadalupe that everyone notices."

Once the secret hideaway of actress Olivia de Havilland, the ranch encourages independence in its visitors' approach to this retreat. "We're very interested in freedom of choice here," comments Ezzell. "We want guests to take control of their own lives. It's up to them to tune into what they need."

The staff offers as much or as little advice and guidance about the various programs as guests want. Guadalupe's objective is to provide an environment and programs conducive to physical, mental and spiritual renewal.

Its comprehensive program, consisting of daily fitness, relaxation, holistic health and recreational activities, is detailed below. Personalized diet and exercise programs are also available.

The percentage of men to women at Guadalupe is about 50/50. Business groups account for the greater-than-usual number of males. (The male/female ratio at most U.S. spas and health retreats is about 1:3.)

The ranch is comfortable for single men and women, married couples and families. A children's program gives parents the freedom to pursue fitness activities while the kids are supervised and entertained.

Guadalupe River Ranch is a perfect romantic getaway or an escape for weary fast-trackers. Unfortunately, this idyllic ranch is too costly for an "affordable" week-long stay, according to the pricing standards of this book. However, it offers reasonably priced weekend packages (approximately $400 a person, double occupancy, including all meals, activities and accommodations).

Activities & Services

Aerobics, yoga, nutritional counseling, weight loss programs, reflexology massage, rolfing, stress management seminars, steam room, sauna, European beauty treatments, swimming, Jacuzzi, tennis, horseback riding, hay rides,

AFFORDABLE SPAS

canoeing, river tubing, hiking, volleyball.

Lodging

Guest rooms are located in quaint stone bungalows with patios or screened porches. Each bungalow bears the name of such famous free thinkers as Will Rogers, Georgia O'Keefe and Carl Jung. As a special touch, each room has fresh-cut flowers.

Cuisine

The beautiful dining room in the main house features a beamed ceiling, fireplace and an adjoining plant-filled solarium. Vegetarian diet and nondiet food is served; calorie intake depends on the person. Not all guests are on diets. The menu includes some southwestern and Tex-Mex dishes, such as fajitas and jalapeno cornbread.

Guadalupe River Ranch and Health Enhancement Center
P.O. Box 929
Boerne, TX 78006   512-698-1592

LAKE AUSTIN RESORT SPA

Austin, Texas

$$
Open: Year-round

Lake Austin Resort Spa is ideal for weight loss and fitness. It also offers something else: a chance to make lasting friendships. "On Sunday night, fifty strangers arrive," says Program Coordinator Sherion Shroeder. "By the end of the week, they're all best friends. A lot of them come back together the following year."

Located on Lake Austin in rolling hill country, the spa is surrounded by a breathtaking profusion of wildflowers during the spring and summer. Originally built as a fishing lodge, Lake Austin had several incarnations, including a nudist colony and a fat farm, before it opened as a resort spa in 1983.

Although men are encouraged to attend, the spa mostly attracts women — mothers and daughters, professionals and homemakers. As a result, the atmosphere feels like a sorority, Texas-style — big fun and lots of hard work.

Each day, guests can choose different exercise classes, relaxation therapies (e.g., massage) and lectures on such subjects as psychological well-being and nutrition. All programs and classes are voluntary.

Regardless of whether a guest is slim and trim or is battling the bulge, everyone fits in. Guests set their own pace. Exercise classes are tailored to one's ability, from beginners to advanced. Guests can request nutritional and fitness counseling and assessment.

Lake Austin requires a seven-night stay. On the last day, guests attend a "Take Us Home" lecture, which reviews everything they've learned during their week at the spa. In addition, everyone receives a packet containing nutrition and exercise tips, recipes and more.

Lake Austin offers special spa theme weeks, such as "Executive Renewal" and "The Man in Your Life." Special spa packages are also available.

Activities & Services

Aerobics (to the rhythm of country western music), stretch and tone (flexercise), circuit training (a combination of aerobics and weights), aquacise, walks, stretching for relaxation, massage, facials, body scrub, beauty makeovers, color consultation, manicures, pedicures, full-service beauty salon, nutritional and fitness counseling and assessment. Health-related lectures and films, cooking classes. Swimming, Jacuzzi, parcourse, weight room, paddle boats.

Lodging

Guest rooms are simple and immaculate. Many boast beautiful lake views.

AFFORDABLE SPAS

Cuisine

900 to 1,200 calories a day. Popular dishes include enchiladas, Mexican-stuffed potatoes, apple-glazed Cornish hen and apple bran muffins.

Lake Austin Resort
1705 Quinlan Park Road
Austin, TX 78732

512-266-2444
800-847-5637 (out of state)

VIRGINIA

HARTLAND HEALTH CENTER

Rapidan, Virginia

$$$
Open: Year-round

The plantation housing the Hartland Health Center is situated on 700 acres of beautiful Virginia countryside, with five small lakes, the Rapidan River and hardwood forests nearby. Cedar Mountain serves as the scenic backdrop for this health retreat.

The emphasis at Hartland Health Center is to work toward the prevention and treatment of chronic degenerative diseases, such as high blood pressure or high cholesterol levels. The center also teaches guests motivation and self-worth through holistic philosophies.

All programs and activities are coed and individually designed. An extensive medical history and series of tests are administered to each guest upon arrival.

A typical day starts at 6:30 AM with a weigh-in and check of vital signs. Breakfast at the Hartland is plentiful. The staff of two physicians and six nurses believes that a high-energy early meal starts the day off right.

Breakfast is followed by a meditation period, after which guests participate in calisthenics.

SOUTHERN SPAS

Lunch is a larger meal, while the evening meal is light. The staff believes most calories should be consumed and burned off earlier in the day.

Approximately 70 percent of the guests are women; the average age is about 50. Hartland has recently started a ten-day program geared toward younger people, but most guests take advantage of the complete 25-day visit. Shorter-term visitors are charged a daily rate of $130.

The atmosphere at Hartland is very relaxed, and those new to health-oriented vacations feel at home. However, this isn't the place for athletes or people seeking fun and frolic. The pace here is slow and steady.

The center is operated by a Seventh-Day Adventist institution. The program, however, is nondenominational and welcomes people of any spiritual orientation.

Activities and Services

Complete history and physical, resting electrocardiogram, treadmill fitness evaluation, blood chemistry analysis, body composition, exercise counseling, group stress management classes, medical lectures, physical therapy, hydrotherapy, cooking school, 15 miles of walking trails, lap pool, exercise room with stationary bikes and treadmills, aquacise, sauna, steam room, contrast showers (alternating hot and cold streams of water that increase circulation), hot packs, massage. Visits to local points of interest, such as Monticello, Civil War battlefields, Shenandoah caverns and the Blue Ridge Mountains.

Lodging

The center's Georgian mansion is decorated in traditional Williamsburg style. Private and shared rooms feature high ceilings, crown moldings and quaint decor. A new facility houses 30 guests at a time, while eight to ten guests can stay in the mansion.

■ AFFORDABLE SPAS

Cuisine

The center offers a total vegetarian diet to achieve a low-fat, high-energy nutritional plan. Fruits, grains, nuts and vegetables are prepared to maintain and accentuate the natural flavors of the food. Sample dishes are vegetarian pizza, "better burgers" (made from oats) and banana dessert smoothies.

Hartland Health Center
P.O. Box 1
Rapidan, VA 22733   703-672-3100

THE HOMESTEAD

Hot Springs, Virginia   **$$$**
Open: Year-round

The Homestead is old-world elegance at its best. Rich with history, it's a 15,000-acre resort paradise, cloistered by the central ranges of the Allegheny Mountains.

It's a spa in the true sense of the word — offering an exhilirating hydrotherapy treatment, known as "the cure." The hottest spring supplying the baths is 106 degrees; the coolest 102.5 degrees. The combined water reaches the baths at 104 degrees. A physician's prescription is needed to take the hottest waters because of the health risk of plunging the body in water at that temperature.

Most guests prefer the indoor bath treatments of a warm tub, sauna, salt glow rub and Scotch shower (where a spa attendant rinses the salt from your body with two pulsating hoses). All bath services are a la carte and appointments are required.

Spa treatments usually are taken at the end of a day of outdoor recreation. Golf reigns supreme here and is played year-round, weather permitting. Pro-golfer Sam Snead has a home in Hot Springs and a tavern named in his honor filled with golf memorabilia (and those famous Stetson straw hats).

Originally built in 1766, The Homestead is steeped in tradition. One anecdote tells of George Washington and Thomas Jefferson riding there to take the waters. The original hotel served as a haven for Confederate soldiers, and General Lee and his wife frequently used the therapeutic waters.

In the 1930s, The Homestead was frequented by America's socialites, with the likes of Mrs. Cornelius Vanderbilt using the hotel as a summer home and hosting lavish parties. It's also been a favorite getaway for presidents and cabinet members. In 1967, then-President Lyndon Johnson visited The Homestead for the first time and exclaimed "My God, what a spread!"

A Homestead vacation focuses on luxury. The service is impeccable, with one staff member (1,000 in all) per guest. This isn't the place where guests live in their sweat suits and nibble on carrots. Daytime dress is sporty and casual, but at night, guests put on the Ritz. Women in cocktail dresses and men in the required jacket and tie dance nightly to the music of a ballroom/dining room orchestra. It's an environment of elegance.

Activities & Services

Combination and mineral baths, massage, salt glow rubs, Scotch showers, full-service beauty salon, exercise room with weight equipment, golf, tennis, archery, bowling, trout fishing, hiking (picnic lunches may be ordered), horseback riding, ice skating, lawn bowling, skeet and trap shooting, skiing, surrey rides, swimming, horseshoes, croquet, volleyball, limousine service, babysitting, physician consultations, nightly films, shopping at Cottage Row and hotel boutiques.

■ AFFORDABLE SPAS

Lodging

The Homestead is a five-star hotel with 604 guest rooms, some with fireplaces. All are elegantly decorated and equipped with every amenity from toiletries to mints placed on guests' pillows every evening. A newer addition offers contemporary comfort yet maintains the grand service and old-world charm.

Cuisine

This is a difficult place to diet or count calories. The food is incredible, and guests on the American plan have all meals included in the price of lodging. The resort has nine restaurants. Dinner in the main dining room is elegant, featuring such entrees as veal stuffed with pork and sage, and filet mignon in brown sauce. The Casino's luncheon buffets are also very popular.

The Homestead
Hot Springs, VA 24445
703-839-5500

800-542-5734 (VA)
800-336-5771 (out of state)

WEST VIRGINIA

COOLFONT RESORT

Berkeley Springs, West Virginia

$ and $$
Open: Year-round

Coolfont is an ideal resort for couples or families with different vacation goals in mind. It offers both spa programs and mountain resort activities. One person can attend exercise classes and self-improvement seminars while a significant other fishes or takes a hike. One person can spend the afternoon lifting weights while another takes a siesta. Everyone at Coolfont coexists peacefully—from the most energetic spa-goer to the most sedentary vacationer.

The 1,200-acre West Virginia resort offers an array of spa programs, ranging from a five-day health retreat plan to a stop-smoking program. Participation in classes and activities is voluntary.

Located between Cacapon Mountain and Warm Springs Ridge near Berkeley Springs, the densely wooded resort boasts a good staff/guest ratio (2:5). Approximately 75 percent of the guests are women between the ages of 30 and 50. Although most guests are serious about weight loss, Coolfont isn't the sort of place that attracts exercise fanatics.

Coolfont's fitness program can have lasting benefits. Unlike some spa programs, Coolfont's program is easy for guests to continue after they return home because it doesn't involve elaborate or expensive equipment.

To all those spa and resort benefits, add a healthy dose of culture. Coolfont's fine arts program includes performances by a string trio, painting classes by an artist-in-residence, cultural films and lectures. As a special touch, classical music is piped into the dining room.

Activities & Services

Morning stretching, body strengthening, aerobics, self-improvement seminars, weight control programs, stress management workshops, wake-up walk, yoga, health education lectures, massage workshops (popular with couples, who learn how to give each other a massage), hot tub, sauna, tennis, hiking, fishing, horseback riding, nature walks, square dancing, swimming, boating, ice skating, cross-country skiing, concerts, art classes, films.

Lodging

Twenty-three rooms are available in the Woodland House Lodge. Rental homes, cabins and campsites set back in the woods are also available.

■ AFFORDABLE SPAS

Cuisine

Diet and nondiet food is available (no set daily calorie count). Low-calorie offerings include stir fry, chicken scampi and cheese enchiladas. A lavish nightly buffet is a big hit with non-dieters, but can be tortuous for calorie counters. Alcohol is available.

Coolfont Resort
Route 1
Cold Run Valley Road
Berkeley Springs, WV 25411

304-258-4500
800-424-1232 (Washington, D.C., area)

THE GREENBRIER

White Sulphur Springs, West Virginia

$$$

Open: Year-round

The luxurious Greenbrier has been in operation since 1858, when it was the largest and most magnificent hotel in the South. However, people had been coming to "take the waters" of White Sulphur Springs since the 1700s.

Rich with history, The Greenbrier served as a headquarters and hospital for the Confederate Army during the Civil War. After the war, the hotel reopened and was the home of General Robert E. Lee and his family until 1870.

In 1987, The Greenbrier opened the doors to its new, multimillion dollar Spa and Mineral Baths where guests still "take the waters," but now also enjoy European-style spa treatments and state-of-the-art exercise facilities.

The natural mineral baths use water from White Sulphur Springs and Alvon Springs, which is similar in mineral composition to the waters of Perrier, France. Water temperature is regulated to guest preference. Separate men's and women's bath facilities ensure privacy.

SOUTHERN SPAS

Greenbrier guests can use the spa facilities on an a la carte basis or participate in one of the specially designed vacation package plans, offered from January 3 to April 1. One package is the five-night "Midweek Spa Vacation" (approximately $1,150), which includes massages, facial, exercise program and classes. Also included are specialized beauty treatments and Greenbrier spa beauty products, a Greenbrier exercise suit, complimentary golf, indoor tennis, cross-country skiing, daily juice breaks and breakfast and dinner daily in the main dining room.

Activities & Services

Mineral baths, soak tubs, Thalasso tubs for underwater massage, whirlpool baths, Swiss shower, Scotch spray, steam, sauna, Swedish and aromatherapy massage, body wraps, European facials, exercise studio with ballet bars and impact-resistant floor, low-impact aerobics, yoga, deck pool-side beverage service, jogging and walking trails, parcourse, full-service beauty salon, body buff with a European seaweed gel, loofah body scrub, talc rub, herbal foam whirlpool, golf, tennis, bowling, cross-country skiing, outdoor ice skating, concerts, evening movies, happy hour, live evening music, dancing.

Lodging

Accommodations in this five-star hotel are spacious and luxurious. Famous for its European service, The Greenbrier treats guests to graciousness and Southern hospitality such as turning down guests' beds each night.

Cuisine

Chefs at The Greenbrier prepare fabulous meals that are pleasing to the eye as well as to the palate. Guests can dine in several of the resort's restaurants or in the elegant main dining room. Spa guests are treated to the specially prepared lighter fare dishes.

■ AFFORDABLE SPAS

The Greenbrier
White Sulphur Springs, WV 24986

304-536-1110
800-624-6070

THE WOODS FITNESS INSTITUTE

Hedgesville, West Virginia

$ or $$
Open: Year-round

The Woods Fitness Institute offers a sophisticated, anti-fad diet and exercise program for people who are serious about losing weight. Located on the grounds of The Woods, a year-round resort in West Virginia's Eastern Panhandle, the institute is only 90 minutes from Washington, D.C., and Baltimore.

Upon arrival, guests are given a comprehensive fitness evaluation to determine coronary risk, blood chemistry, blood pressure, lung capacity, muscle strength, body fat and overall flexibility. Throughout their stay, guests measure their progress against the results from their first fitness evaluation.

The institute concentrates almost exclusively on fitness and dieting. Weekend and week-long programs are available. The institute also offers a month-long weight loss program that allows guests to shed the pounds slowly.

"If you start out slowly and at your own pace, you are much more likely to continue with the program once you get home," says Assistant Director Dee Blackstone.

The resort attracts couples and families. However, most of the institute's guests are female. Spa-goers frequently take time out from the program to enjoy recreational activities and sight-seeing highlights, such as Harpers Ferry (Thomas Jefferson's favorite town), Fort Frederick and Shepherdstown (the oldest town in West Virginia). The Woods adjoins the 23,000-acre Sleepy Creek State Forest with its miles of hiking trails and streams.

SOUTHERN SPAS

Activities & Services

Aquacise, weight training, stretching, aerobic dance, whirlpool, sauna, massage. Lectures on nutrition, exercise, stress management, lifestyle changes. Walks to scenic or historic points of interest, swimming, tennis, racquetball, softball, volleyball, basketball, films, fishing, ice skating. Nearby cross-country skiing, golf and canoeing.

Lodging

Moderately priced guest rooms with decks overlooking the pond or pool are available. Some Evergreen Lodge rooms that cost a little more include a whirlpool bath, fireplace and balcony overlooking a pine forest. A-frame cabins with fireplace, deck, two bedrooms and kitchen are also available. Guests staying for a month can rent "fitness cottages" at reduced rates.

Cuisine

Each guest is served 1,000 calories a day in the inn's Walden Dining Room. Among the low-fat, high-carbohydrate dishes served are Swiss caraway chicken, stuffed flounder and rock Cornish game hen. Red meat is served twice a week in small portions.

The Woods Fitness Institute
P.O. Box 5
Hedgesville, WV 25427

304-754-7977
800-248-2222

CHAPTER 4

Midwestern Spas and Fitness Resorts

4

ILLINOIS

THE HEARTLAND

Gilman, Illinois

$$$/Weekends
Open: Year-round

The name of this spa is apt. It really feels like the heartland of America. Befittingly, The Heartland offers guests some of the most solid and professional spa programs around—based on scientific research. Everyone from the spa director to the aerobics instructors can discuss the latest research findings.

Located about two hours south of Chicago on a country estate, The Heartland is surrounded by a lake and farmland reminiscent of a Grandma Moses painting. On early morning walks, guests wander through cornfields, woods and farmyards where they see the whole cast of barnyard characters—pigs with piglets, horses, goats, cows and more.

A typical day at The Heartland might begin with a morning stretch and walk, followed by race walking or "Heartbeat" (light to intermediate exercise). (During the winter, the walk is replaced with cross-country skiing, conditions permitting.) The morning ends with "Waterworks" (pool exercises).

Afternoon activities might include a lecture, "Major Motion" (advanced aerobics) or free weights, followed by muscle training and yoga. After dinner, guests take an evening walk and attend another lecture on subjects such as stress management.

Needless to say, guests can't participate in everything. In fact, The Heartland staff encourages them to set their own pace.

In between all those activities, guests can pamper themselves by scheduling a massage, sauna, facial or other beauty treatment.

An excellent nutritionist is on hand to answer guests' diet questions and determine their body fat content. However, The Heartland isn't a fat farm. Most guests aren't overweight and are more concerned with managing stress than with shedding pounds. Most guests lose a few pounds, anyway, by just sticking to The Heartland diet.

The spa accommodates 27 guests at a time. It attracts a lot of professionals from Chicago and couples who want to shape up together. It's also popular with frequent spa-goers who've experienced a lot of spa programs and know a good one when they see it.

The Heartland is too expensive by this book's pricing standards for a week-long stay (approximately $1,290, double occupancy, seven nights). However, the weekend program fits within our price range (approximately $360, double occupancy for two nights; includes all meals, transportation from Chicago, tips and most activities).

The Heartland is ideal for a spontaneous getaway (reservations permitting). Because it provides practically all the clothing spa-goers need—bathrobe, shorts, t-shirts, socks, sweat suits and jackets—guests only need to pack a toothbrush and running shoes.

MIDWESTERN SPAS

Activities & Services

Race walking, yoga, resistance conditioning, all levels of aerobics, free weights, supercircuit (a workout on an entire set of special equipment), pool swimming and "Waterworks," running track, parcourse, tennis, hiking, cross-country skiing, lectures, massage, facials, manicure, pedicure, hairstyling, makeup and color consultation, steam rooms, rock saunas, whirlpools.

Lodging

The rooms are small and tidy with twin beds. The bathrooms are larger than one would expect and stocked with ample shampoo, conditioner, hand and body lotion and a hair dryer.

Cuisine

For women, an 1,100- to 1,200-calorie menu is served; for men, a 1,500-calorie menu is served. Portions are generous, almost hearty: big bowls of gazpacho, meatless enchiladas, grilled salmon steak, granola and bran muffins. Fruit is always on hand for snacking.

The Heartland
Gilman, Illinois

Direct all correspondence and phone inquiries to The Heartland business office:

18 East Chestnut Street, Suite 200
Chicago, IL 60611   312-266-2050

INDIANA

THE SPA AT FRENCH LICK SPRINGS GOLF AND TENNIS RESORT

French Lick, Indiana

$$/Winter
$$$/Spring, Summer, Fall
Open: Year-round

The grand old French Lick Springs Resort, built in 1809, is undergoing a $3 million face-lift that will restore it to its original Victorian elegance. Paddle fans, verandas, beautiful moldings, mill work, French doors and elegant gardens help re-create the splendor of a bygone era.

Located on 2,600 acres of green lawns and wooded hillsides, French Lick Springs has all the amenities of an expensive spa, but at more reasonable rates, especially during winter when prices are reduced by 50 percent.

The spa features a number of different reasonably priced spa packages. "People in lower paying jobs deserve to be pampered and spoiled as much as those earning more money," says Gail Spencer, spa director. All spa packages include deluxe hotel accommodations, low-calorie meals, exercise classes and beauty services (e.g., facial, manicure), stress management workshops and other activities.

A typical day might begin with a 7 AM walk, jog or aquacise in the dome pool. That might be followed by a sauna, whirlpool or mineral bath (fed by Pluto's Spring) and a massage. Six different types of massage are offered including lymph drainage, purported to be effective against acne and cellulite.

Afternoon classes are designed to improve flexibility and strengthen the heart, lungs and muscles. After that, a guest might opt for a European skincare treatment that helps cleanse, stimulate and normalize the complexion.

Every day guests receive a schedule card of spa activities. They are expected to show up, says Spencer, even though participation is voluntary. Most people take part in all of the exercise classes, which aren't overly rigorous.

The spa attracts a lot of working women between the ages of 30 and 45, in addition to affluent homemakers. About half of them are serious about losing weight; the other half come to French Lick Springs for the fun of it — and the opportunity to be pampered.

A major golf and tennis resort, French Lick Springs has 525 rooms. But to guarantee guests plenty of personal attention, the spa program only accommodates 24 people at a time. With a 16-member staff, the spa boasts one of the best staff/guest ratios in the business.

A wide range of recreational activities and an excellent children's program make French Lick Springs an ideal vacation spot for families.

Activities & Services

Aquacise, aerobics, body tone and firm, stretching, dance, walks. Reflexology, aromatherapy, Swedish massage, lymph drainage. Facials, skincare analysis, European skincare treatments, makeup application lesson, full-service beauty salon. Stress management programs. Mineral bath, sauna, indoor/outdoor whirlpool, swimming, golf, tennis, skeet and trap shooting, horseback riding, bowling, miniature golf, bicycling, surrey rides, playground, miniature train ride, wading pool, billiards, skiing, live nightly entertainment, films, dancing. Fishing and sailing at nearby Patoka Lake.

Lodging

Spa-goers stay in deluxe suites or double rooms in the French Lick Springs Resort. Rooms are decorated in soothing, muted colors.

Cuisine

Of French Lick's six restaurants, two serve a special 1,200-calorie-a-day spa menu. However, it's up to the

AFFORDABLE SPAS

guests to stick to the spa menu. (Spencer suspects that most people cheat a little and indulge in the resort's regular cuisine.) Sample dishes from the spa cuisine are shrimp shishkabob, teriyaki chicken and vegetarian meals. Alcohol is available, but not recommended for dieters.

The Spa at French Lick Springs
Golf and Tennis Resort   812-935-9381
French Lick, IN 47432   800-457-4042

MICHIGAN

WEIGHT WATCHERS AT THE BARTLEY HOUSE

$$
Open: Late June to Early November

Harbor Springs, Michigan

One of the most tried and true weight loss programs around, Weight Watchers is the diet and fitness approach one finds at The Bartley House, an English Tudor mansion located on the grounds of Boyne Highland's Resort.

Focusing on Weight Watchers' diet, daily exercise and motivational workshops, guests are assisted by a very supportive staff—most of whom were once overweight themselves. Upon request, the staff can develop an exercise program based on an individual's needs and lifestyle.

Guests have the option of participating in as many or as few of the daily exercise classes as they like. Classes range from light aerobics to yoga. However, everyone is encouraged to participate in at least one or two daily fitness classes, which shouldn't tax even the most inactive guests. Most classes are suitable for beginners.

Because education and group support are important components of the Weight Watchers' program, part of the day is devoted to lectures, classes and workshops. Subjects include planning menus, increasing willpower, learning assertiveness and reducing stress.

The program is designed for anyone who wants to lose weight and learn a new and better way of eating. Most guests are women. However, the program is also popular with couples or friends who enjoy helping each other achieve a common goal.

Located in the scenic Michigan north country, the spa gives guests the opportunity to combine tourist activities with the Weight Watchers' program. Guests can take a leisurely drive through picturesque countryside to the Mackinac Bridge, shop in nearby Petosky and Harbor Springs, visit quaint harbor towns or hike along Lake Michigan and Little Traverse Bay.

Activities & Services

Aerobics, aquacise, stretch and tone (flexercise), yoga, lectures and behavior modification workshops, personal exercise programs, nutritional counseling, group support sessions, swimming, sauna, walks, golf, tennis, hiking.

Lodging

Accommodations are standard. However, the lobby of The Bartley House is reminiscent of a Scandanavian ski lodge, with a large stone hearth and an upstairs loft area ringing the large room. The ski lodge design is no accident. The Bartley House doubles as a ski lodge during the winter months when its spa program is closed.

Cuisine

1,000 calories a day. Sample dishes include poached salmon with sauce verte, linguine with bay scallops and zucchini, vichyssoise and honeyed pumpkin custard.

Weight Watchers at The Bartley House
Hedrick Road
Harbor Springs, MI 49740

■ AFFORDABLE SPAS

For more information on the program at The Bartley House and other Weight Watchers' spa programs, contact

Weight Watchers Resorts and Spas   313-443-1414
15815 W. 12 Mile Road   800-LEANER-U
Southfield, MI 48076   800-826-5088 (Canada)

MINNESOTA

BIRDWING SPA

Litchfield, Minnesota $$ **Open: Year-round**

If breakfast in bed is your idea of stress reduction, you'll love Birdwing. After breakfast, the program becomes a little more rigorous, but not by much. Pampering plays a major role at this spa.

A typical day might include a walk around the grounds of this wildlife sanctuary, aerobics toning class, facial, yoga stretch class, sauna and massage. Evening activities range from cooking classes to a lecture and film.

All activities are voluntary. Upon arrival, guests are privately weighed and measured, a diet history is taken (food allergies, meal preferences, etc.) and counseling is offered. The dietician and fitness instructor work together to design a personalized program for each guest.

If a guest comes to the spa just to relax, and to diet, he or she can skip the preliminary counseling and choose which classes to attend.

Birdwing offers day, weekend and week-long spa packages. The weekend program is less structured because it tends to attract fast-trackers who put in too much time at the office that week and need to relax. During the week, Birdwing primarily attracts women, between the ages of 30 and 60, who want to lose weight.

Located on Star Lake, the nine-bedroom Tudor spa is the former estate of a Minnesota executive, who filled it with beautiful Ethan Allen furnishings. The spa's 300 acres are a bird watcher's paradise—hence the name Birdwing.

Activities & Services

Slimnastics, aerobics, yoga, dancercise, back strengthening exercises, walks, aquacise, massage, reflexology, facial, tanning booth, manicure, pedicure. Lectures on such subjects as nutrition, cardiac health, stress management. Fitness and dietary counseling, swimming, bicycling, sauna, Jacuzzi, canoeing, bird watching and cross-country skiing.

Lodging

For a special treat, there's a master suite with private bath, fireplace and Jacuzzi. Other accommodations are single and double rooms with shared bath.

Cuisine

950 to 1,100 calories a day. Dishes include veal asparagus rolls, butterscotch brownies (85 calories), chicken tacos with salsa.

Birdwing Spa
Rural Route 2, Box 99
Litchfield, MN 55355   612-693-6064

OHIO

SANS SOUCI HEALTH RESORT

$$$

Bellbrook, Ohio   **Open: May to October**

The program at Sans Souci blends European spa traditions with American know-how. Upon arrival, guests meet individually with Suzanne Kircher, the Rumanian-born spa director and owner, to discuss medical history, lifestyle, food preferences and spa goals.

Most guests come to Sans Souci specifically to lose weight. However, dieting is only one part of the program. Guests also learn low-calorie cooking techniques, proper food combinations, and how to outsmart constant hunger, break food addictions and control weight through behavior modification.

Some spas have guests exercising at the crack of dawn. Sans Souci is more civilized—part of the European touch. Rising time is 7:45 AM. Instead of exercising immediately—guests are served a glass of lemon water in their rooms. That is followed by stretching, breathing and wake-up exercises. Following breakfast, guests take a walk on the parcourse and participate in a small group discussion.

The rest of the day consists of more exercise classes, pool classes, yoga, massage and beauty treatments (such as a facial). Some evenings, guests listen to a lecture, given by experts in such areas as stress management, behavioral modification or fashion.

Surrounded by green lawns and 80 acres of pine forest, Sans Souci is decorated in English country style, with lots of chintz upholstery and quaint furniture. The spa only accepts seven guests at a time, thus guaranteeing personal attention. Because this is such a popular place, reservations must be made well in advance.

Equally popular are European spa vacations organized by Kircher that combine gourmet dieting with sight-seeing. Among the tours are a visit to Champney's—the premier health resort in Great Britain—and trips to Incosol, a luxurious resort in Spain on the Costa del Sol.

Activities & Services

Aerobics, aquacise, yoga, T'ai Chi, slimnastics, walks, race walking, meditation, stretching, breathing and wake-up exercises, dance, 18-station parcourse, massage, facials, herbal wraps, manicures, pedicures, hairstyling, color coordination. Classes and lectures on subjects such as osteoporosis and the latest findings in weight control. Cooking demonstrations, swimming, Jacuzzi.

Lodging

Sans Souci's lovely rooms are decorated in a traditional style with private bath and separate dressing area.

Cuisine

800 calories a day are served. A one-day juice fast is recommended for the first day. Dishes include eggwhite omelette, seafood divan, fruit-garnished chicken. Dinner is served by candlelight to classical music. Picnic lunch trips are also available.

Sans Souci Health Resort
3745 Route 725
Bellbrook, OH 45305   513-848-4851

OKLAHOMA

AKIA
$
Sulphur, Oklahoma   **Open: Spring and Fall**

Several years ago, Wilhelmina Maguire visited one of the most respected spas in the country. Maguire loved everything about that state-of-the-art spa—the programs, the setting, the results—everything, that is, except the (gulp) price tag—more than $2,500 a week per person!

Nonetheless, she was inspired by what she'd seen. Teaming up with Jeanne Meyer, Maguire decided to open a moderately priced spa. In 1985, they founded Akia, which may not offer all the plush amenities of a "super spa," but promises the same results: substantial weight loss (seven to ten pounds a week), improved physical fitness and significant stress reduction.

Adjacent to Chickasaw National Recreation Area in the Arbuckle Mountains, this women-only spa seems like a combination of summer camp and boot camp, with its rigorous, up-at-the-crack-of-dawn schedule, woodsy environment and rustic cottages.

Late sleepers may find Akia's 6 AM rising time hard to handle. Each morning begins with a stretching session on the redwood deck and a two-mile hike. The hike is followed by an hour of body toning in a pavilion by a lake.

Finally, breakfast is served, but it's nothing to get too worked up over — cereal with fruit and juice. Lunch consists of a high-fiber protein shake. Period.

Guests seldom make good on threats to sneak into town for a hamburger and fries, or drop out of the more strenuous activities. During the first few days, one hears a lot of good-natured moaning and groaning. But the agony quickly becomes the ecstasy as the pounds start to fall away.

Activities & Services

Aerobics, body contouring, relaxation exercises, massage, facial, personal color analysis, body composition, nutritional counseling, walking, bicycling, hot tub, lectures on subjects such as nutrition for life, low-calorie product selection and techniques for defatting.

Lodging

Akia's newly restored native rock cottages offer comfortable and simple accommodations. The spa also features a large deck and courtyard for lounging and sunning. A wood-frame duplex is also available.

Cuisine

800 to 1,000 calories a day, consisting of the breakfast and lunch described above plus a light three- to four-course dinner. Akia's ethnic dishes are very popular with guests.

Akia
2316 Northwest 45th Place
Oklahoma City, OK 73112   405-842-6269

WISCONSIN

INTERLAKEN RESORT AND COUNTRY SPA
West Lake Geneva, Wisconsin $$$
                                          Open: Year-round

Located on a hill overlooking lush green countryside and Lake Como, the 90-acre Interlaken spa resort is a favorite family vacation spot. It features activities for children, and outdoor recreation and spa facilities for adults. The resort's fully equipped spa specializes in weight loss, cardiorespiratory development and pampering.

Interlaken, like most resort spas, gives guests a chance to combine health and recreational activities, enjoying a little or a lot of both. Some guests are serious about losing weight and working out; others are more interested in playing golf or tennis.

Guests can sign up for specific spa classes or services — such as aerobics, aquacise, massage and hydrotherapy. They can firm and improve muscle tone through body sculpting, under the supervision of Dr. Val Vallese (the trainer for 1987's Mr. Universe).

Many spa-goers participate in one of Interlaken's three- or five-day "Spa Escape Packages." Those packages focus on either starting an exercise program or expanding and improving an existing one. The spa staff tailors a fitness program to an individual's needs. Everything — from exer-

AFFORDABLE SPAS

cise classes and beauty services to meals and accommodations — is included in the package price.

Activities & Services

Aerobics, aquacise, stretch and tone (flexercise), weight training, massage, facials, hand and foot treatments, herbal wraps, makeup application lesson, full-service beauty salon, mineral bath, suntanning studio, hydrotherapy whirlpool, steam room, sauna, swimming, sailing, waterskiing, game arcade, tennis, golf nearby, horseback riding, snowmobiling, skiing.

Lodging

The rooms, like the resort itself, are modern and comfortable. Family-size villas with kitchens are also available for a slightly higher price.

Cuisine

The Lake Bluff dining room serves nondiet food, as well as low-calorie entrees. Guests who want to lose weight can request the spa menu, which indicates calorie counts for each item. It's recommended that dieters not exceed 1,200 calories a day; however, that's up to the individual. Sample dishes are salmon Florentine, petite filet mignon, pancakes with cottage cheese and strawberries.

Interlaken Resort and Country Spa
Route 2, Box 80
Highway 50   414-248-9121
West Lake Geneva, WI 53147   800-225-5558

OLYMPIA VILLAGE CONFERENCE CENTER RESORT SPA

Oconomowoc, Wisconsin

$$ and $$$
Open: Year-round

Olympia Village is a modern mega-resort with 400 rooms, 400 acres and a mind-boggling assortment of services and activities. Its excellent spa program boasts lots of professionally executed beauty and pampering services.

Olympia features several different spa packages and a number of specials, such as its two-night "Spa Sampler" package — a perfect introduction into the spa world for the uninitiated. Guests sample a little of everything: three diet meals a day, a massage and facial, six exercise classes, makeup application lesson and accommodations.

The "Four-Night Retreat" plan and the "Seven-Night Renewal" plan offer more of the above activities. The plans also feature a diet and fitness program that uses behavior modification and is tailored to each individual's needs and abilities. Olympia provides guests with a follow-up regimen to take home.

The spa attracts more women than men, and the clientele has changed in recent years. "When we first started out six years ago, the guests were less serious about health and fitness," says Assistant Spa Director Lois Thiede. "Quite a few were wealthy women with a lot of time on their hands. But now the people are much more interested in nutrition and fitness, and we get a lot more working women."

Set in Wisconsin's famed lake country, Olympia is a year-round vacation land, surrounded by forest, hills, rivers and lakes. In addition to the spa facilities, there are all sorts of other temptations: golf, polo games, films, horseback riding, dancing, sailing, trips to nearby Old World Wisconsin and fishing, to name a few. After dark, the agenda includes night clubs and live entertainment.

With its many and varied features, Olympia offers a practical solution to families and couples with different ideas about how to spend their vacation.

■ AFFORDABLE SPAS

Activities & Services

(Excluding recreational activities mentioned above): Gymnastics, aquacise, aerobics, stretching, water ballet, walks, weight-lifting, problem spot exercises, 12-station gym, free weights, yoga, massage, facials, loofah body scrub, herbal wrap, individual mineral bath, scalp treatment, full-service beauty salon, Roman pools, steam rooms, saunas, whirlpools, swimming.

Lodging

Spa-goers stay in a quiet wing of the Olympia Village Hotel. The newly remodeled rooms afford lake views. (Smoking is prohibited in the rooms.)

Cuisine

Stick to the spa dining room and you'll never consume more than 600 to 1,200 calories a day. Try Olympia Village's other restaurants and kiss your diet goodbye. Sample items from the spa menu are lobster pasta salad and hearts of palm and mushroom pizza.

Olympia Village Conference Center Resort Spa
1350 Royal Mile Road 414-567-0311
Oconomowoc, WI 53066 800-558-9573

THE WOODEN DOOR

$

Lake Geneva, Wisconsin

Open: January, and April to October

The Wooden Door is a spa with a sense of humor. Its very name is a pun on a famous luxury spa. Even the exercise classes have humorous names, such as "Moan and Groan" and "Lean and Mean."

Humor aside, The Wooden Door is affordable and refreshingly realistic. "We're not in the business of telling women what they should look like," says part owner Naomi Stark. "There's no goofiness, no silliness, but a down-to-earth, relaxing, 'feel good about yourself' atmosphere."

The Wooden Door is a lot like an all-women's camp. The accommodations are rustic. There's no high-tech exercise equipment or steam room. Guests supply their own linens, sleep on steel frame bunk beds (two to four to a cabin) and scrape their own dishes, assuming anything is left on their plates.

Like summer camp, the spa brings out the mischief in some guests. One time a 70-year-old grandmother was discovered leading an entourage of guests to a nearby male strip-tease joint. But most guests stick with the program, which includes strenuous exercise, beauty and relaxation treatments, educational lectures and workshops.

Mornings are devoted primarily to exercise—everything from walking and stretching to dance and aerobics. Some fitness classes are taught in a charming gazebo overlooking the lake.

Afternoon and evening activities include beauty and relaxation treatments, and lectures and workshops on such topics as self-defense, nutrition, self-awareness, time management, business confidence and dressing, and left-brain, right-brain theory.

Located on Lake Geneva, the 54-acre spa boasts beautiful scenery and dazzling lake sunrises that bring to mind the set of *On Golden Pond*.

Many of The Wooden Door's guests are homemakers from the Chicago area who want to lose weight and get in shape. Most guests find the program a rewarding and affordable way to make a fresh start in life. Because of The Wooden Door's popularity, reservations should be booked well in advance.

■ AFFORDABLE SPAS

Activities & Services

Low-impact aerobics, yoga, walks, weight training, stretching, toning, massage, facial, manicure, pedicure, makeup application lesson, fashion coordination, lectures and workshops, bicycling, hiking, sailing, canoeing, waterskiing, swimming, volleyball, jogging, cross-country skiing, popular films. Nearby tennis.

Lodging

Roomy guest cabins have wall-to-wall carpeting, heating, electric lights and a large bathroom with more than enough outlets for everyone's hairdryer. Some have adjoining lounge areas with fireplaces.

Cuisine

1,000 calories a day. Sample dishes are chicken breast with mushroom sauce, herbed rice, zucchini pizza and peaches with yogurt. Eight glasses of water a day are required. Evening snacks include plain popcorn or fruit.

The Wooden Door
Lake Geneva, WI

Mailing address:
P.O. Box 830
Barrington, IL 60010   312-382-2888

CHAPTER 5

Western Spas and Fitness Resorts

5

ARIZONA

LOEWS VENTANA CANYON RESORT

Tucson, Arizona

$$/June to September
$$$/September to June
Open: Year-round

This world-class resort looks like it was lowered from the sky and set in the desert. A superb example of environmental architecture and design, it blends in perfectly with the Santa Catalina Mountains looming directly behind the resort. The dramatic desert landscape—not the resort—becomes the focal point. Even the corners of the 400-room, sepia-toned complex resemble tall, stately cactuses.

The interior is equally impressive. The lobby is decorated in the serene colors of a desert sunset—soft sage, dusty blue, smokey lavendar and pink gold, gently reflected against the bleached stone floor.

The resort's spa, called the Lakeside Spa and Tennis Club, features a program that was designed and is partly supervised by the Tucson Heart Institute. A typical day at the spa, located in a separate building from the resort, might

AFFORDABLE SPAS

include an early morning race walk or mountain bike tour, stretch and flex (flexercise) and heat therapy such as a sauna, Jacuzzi or steambath. After lunch, guests enjoy sunbathing, water aerobics, unstructured time for a massage or beauty salon treatment, tennis and another exercise class. A comprehensive computerized fitness analysis, administered by the Tucson Heart Institute, is also available.

All spa services and activities are offered to resort guests on an a la carte basis. In addition, special spa packages are available throughout the year.

Activities & Services

(In addition to the spa activities mentioned above): 2.5-mile parcourse trail, "The General Manager's Run," "The Morning Workout," one-on-one supervised instruction, Universal and free-weight training equipment, lap swimming, body fat measurement, golf, tennis, art tours, environmental tours, haircare and skincare lectures, cooking demonstrations with resort chefs, free shuttle service to nearby Sabino Canyon.

Lodging

Spacious, balconied guest rooms reflect the sophisticated southwestern theme of the lobby. Terry cloth robes and an assortment of toiletries, such as shampoo and hand lotion, are provided.

Cuisine

Most resorts serve spa food in only one restaurant. Loews Ventana offers superb low-calorie cuisine in all three of its restaurants. The festive, friendly Canyon Cafe, appointed with hand-caned hickory chairs and southwestern decor, serves imaginative diet dishes (no set calorie count), such as whole wheat waffles and pancakes, turkey, apple and champagne sausage, lean roast beef and pasta salad with a soy ginger vinaigrette dressing, and linguine with stir-fried shrimp. For serious gourmands, a three-course low-calorie dinner that changes daily is served in Ventana, an award-winning restaurant. Low-calorie food is also available at the Flying V Bar and Grill. For guests who want to break their diets in style, Ventana's creme brulee is the finest anywhere in the West—maybe even the East for that matter.

Lakeside Spa and Tennis Club
Loews Ventana Canyon Resort
7000 North Resort Drive
Tucson, AZ 85715   602-299-2020

SCOTTSDALE HILTON RESORT AND SPA

Scottsdale, Arizona

$$/Summer
$$$/Spring, Fall, Winter
Open: Year-round

The Scottsdale Hilton looks like the backdrop of a Ralph Lauren ad for the good life in the southwest. Every detail is perfect—from the Spanish adobe architecture, mosaic bell tower and rugged beamed ceilings to the gardens, courtyards and furnishings.

The colors call to mind a soft desert sunset: peach, rose, violet and lilac. Even the spa workout room, while modern in every respect, has rustic bleached wood pillars and red tile.

During the summer the Hilton's rates are reduced by half, making this spa a good bargain. Airfares to Phoenix, the closest major airport, are low in the summer, too.

Not surprisingly, the spa is as attractive as everything else about this resort. Indirect lighting from skylights, the warm wood and pastel hues flatter skin tones. After a visit to the spa, guests never want to work out under artificial lighting again.

The spa program includes aerobics, water exercises, Nautilus training and sports such as tennis, relaxation treat-

AFFORDABLE SPAS

ments such as massage and spa cuisine. The staff is extremely knowledgeable. Ask any one of them to develop a personal exercise and diet plan and they'll be happy to oblige. Everyone gets a lot of attention here.

Says Assistant Spa Director Brandon Hill, "It's not like a health club with a lot of people standing around waiting to use the machines, and socializing to pass the time and forgetting why they're there. Here it's one-on-one and small enough that you get a good workout."

The spa attracts an equal number of men and women, a lot of local professionals, families and some athletes. It's a good place to meet people.

Often the hotel staff organizes guest picnics and tubing outings on Salt River. Those outings aren't an official spa offering. They usually happen spontaneously as the staff becomes friendly with the guests.

Activities & Services

High- and low-impact aerobics, aquacise, free weight room, Nautilus equipment, aerobicycles, stationary bicycles, suntanning solarium, sauna, steam room, massage, facial, whirlpool, tennis, swimming. Nearby hot-air balloon rides, horseback riding, golf and Grand Canyon sight-seeing plane rides.

Lodging

The Hilton features 187 deluxe single and double guest rooms, all beautifully decorated in southwestern colors and some with vaulted wood beam ceilings. Families often stay in the Hilton Villas, with two bedrooms, living room, kitchen and separate swimming area.

Cuisine

Low-calorie food is served in the Iron Horse Grill restaurant. Calorie count is listed next to each item. Sample dishes are fiesta fruit salad, pasta with honey yogurt dressing, broiled fish, steamed vegetable plate. Nondieters should try innovative regional specialties such as the Mazatlan club sandwich. It's just like a traditional club except with a soft tortilla instead of bread, guacamole, cheese and chicken.

Scottsdale Hilton Resort and Spa
6333 North Scottsdale Road
Scottsdale, AZ 85253

602-948-7750
800-HILTONS

TUCSON NATIONAL RESORT AND SPA

Tucson, Arizona

$$$/Off-season, mid-season and special season packages
Open: Year-round

Imagine a desert paradise — pale apricot adobe walls, tinkling fountains, skylights, colorful tile, cool marble floors, bleached beamed ceilings and southwestern furnishings, set in the Arizona landscape. That accurately describes Tucson National Resort, a well-known spa, golf and tennis club.

A typical day at this spa might include low-impact aerobics, stress management, creative movement and water aerobics. The spa offers a wide range of wraps, facials and massage, including the mechanical Orthion multitherapy stretching unit (see Glossary). The latter may not be everyone's idea of relaxation, but it's worth a try for the experience alone.

A professional, low-key staff offers dietary assistance, menu planning, physical evaluation, body composition analysis and weight training programs.

Although in the past most guests have been more interested in golf and tennis than spa activities, that's starting to change. A fully equipped, separate men's spa makes it one of the few resort spas in the country that specifically caters to men.

AFFORDABLE SPAS

During the winter season, prices exceed this book's $1,150 a week limit; however, off-season and mid-season prices and special spa packages make Tucson National Resort and Spa a good value and within the "affordable" pricing standards used for this book.

Activities & Services

Stretch and tone (flexercise), water aerobics, low-impact aerobics, gym with free weights and exercise equipment, body composition, menu planning, nutritional counseling, physical evaluation, stress management seminars, creative movement, behavior modification, health-related lectures, massage, facial, manicure, pedicure, skincare salon, full-service unisex salon, herbal wrap, loofah scrub, salt glow rub, brush and tone, Swiss shower, panthermal, Orthion massage, eucalyptus inhalation rooms, sauna, hydrotherapy pools, tanning beds, Russian bath (a steam room for men only), swimming, walks, tennis, golf, hiking.

Lodging

Lovely, spacious guest rooms include a wet bar, enormous bathroom and dressing room area, artfully decorated with Mexican tile. The ceilings are beamed. Frescoes are painted over shuttered windows. Furnishings and colors are influenced by Mexican and American Indian design. A robe and toiletries, such as hand lotion, are provided.

Cuisine

Low-calorie food is served in the Fiesta dining room. Calorie counts are listed next to each item. The menu changes daily and includes a number of different choices. Sample dishes include watercress soup, fruit sorbet, broiled swordfish, baked apple, cold seafood platter and poached salmon with dill sauce.

WESTERN SPAS

Tucson National Resort and Spa
2727 West Club Drive
Tucson, AZ 85741

602-297-2271
800-528-4856

WEIGHT WATCHERS AT THE CAMELVIEW RADISSON RESORT

Scottsdale, Arizona

$$

Open: Year-round

This Arizona retreat, located on 35 lushly landscaped acres in the the heart of Scottsdale, helps spa-goers trim down with the Weight Watchers' fitness and diet program, which includes exercise, relaxation, motivational workshops and indulging in beauty treatments.

The Camelview's professional staff develops a personalized exercise regimen based on each guest's goals and lifestyle. In addition, they teach guests how to determine their own heart rate and achieve a level of exercise targeted toward a specific heart rate.

Exercise classes are offered throughout the day—everything from stretch and tone (flexercise) to yoga and light aerobics. If guests are out of shape, they won't feel intimidated, thanks to the well-planned beginners' classes and supportive staff (most of them were once overweight and out of shape).

In addition to fitness activities, behavioral change is a major part of the program. Over the years, Weight Watchers has devoted a lot of research to this aspect of the program. As a result, the organization knows what works and how to motivate and inspire people.

Guests spend a lot of time attending workshops, classes and lectures on subjects such as menu planning, controlling stress, maintaining weight loss motivation and assertiveness training.

Because of The Camelview's location, its guests often

AFFORDABLE SPAS

take a break from spa activities long enough to venture into the Arizona desert. Among the popular sight-seeing destinations are Ghost Town (an authentic one used in a western film), Pinnacle Peak and ruins of old Native American settlements. Guests also like to visit the area's museums and shops that feature local handicrafts.

Activities & Services

Aerobics, aquacise, stretch and tone, yoga, lectures and behavior modification workshops, personal exercise program, nutritional counseling, group support sessions, massage, herbal body wrap, loofah body polish, facials, hand and foot massage, manicure, pedicure, makeup application lesson, Jacuzzi, sauna, parcourse, swimming, walks, tennis and nearby golf.

Lodging

Comfortable and nicely decorated guest rooms are located in three wings of the resort. They boast vistas of either the mountains, desert or lakes that surround the property.

Cuisine

1,000 calories a day are served. Sample dishes are red snapper with sesame vegetables, plentiful vegetable and fruit plates, honeyed pumpkin custard.

Weight Watchers at The Camelview Radisson Resort
7601 East Indian Bend Road
Scottsdale, Arizona 85253   602-991-2400

     For more information on The Camelview program and Weight Watchers' four other spa programs, contact

Weight Watchers' Resorts and Spas   313-443-1414
15815 W. 12 Mile Road   800-LEANER-U
Southfield, MI 48076   800-826-5088 (Canada)

CALIFORNIA

BERMUDA INN FITNESS AND REDUCING RESORT

Lancaster, California

$$

Open: Year-round

If you're not sure what aerobics is all about, Bermuda Inn is the spa for you. Many guests haven't done a leg lift since high school. In fact, the spa is ideal for women who've never exercised and would like to start a fitness program they can continue at home. It offers guests a sensible approach to fitness in a very supportive environment.

Most guests lose about a pound a day. They can participate in the full program described below or limit themselves to just part of it. The structured daily schedule gives guests a lot of options. Exercise classes are categorized from moderately active to very active to prevent guests from taking on something too rigorous and getting sore.

At 7 AM, the spa's registered nurse weighs guests and takes their blood pressure. Breakfast usually is followed by a walk and a relaxing stretching class, which is then followed by a cardiorespiratory workout (including monitoring participants' heart rate). Next comes the popular "Sit and Fit" class — exercises one can do while sitting at home, in the office or on a plane. Late-morning fitness activities include aquacise.

After lunch, guests can put their feet up for a one-hour siesta. One afternoon a week, spa-goers can choose to spend that hour consulting with the spa doctor.

Afternoon activities include a number of other exercise classes (listed below). Those who've had enough stretching and toning for one day can take a shopping excursion to Lancaster.

At 4 PM, guests take another walk and then relax for a half-hour before the 5 PM happy hour. That hour is happy,

AFFORDABLE SPAS

not because everyone has a cocktail (alcohol isn't permitted), but because exercise is over for the day and low-calorie hors d'oeuvres are served — a welcome relief for the famished spa-goers. Happy hour conversation is full of comparisons: who's the sorest, who lost the most pounds and inches, and who would go to any extreme for a chance to feast on pizza.

Located in California's Antelope Valley, high desert country about an hour north of Los Angeles, Bermuda Inn looks like a standard motel typically found in that part of California. It's short on elegance and long on weight loss and fitness results.

Activities & Services

Stretching, "Sit and Fit," aquacise, cardiorespiratory workout, toning with light weights, trim and tone (exercises for hips, thighs, stomach), swimming, Jacuzzi, tanning booth, sauna, walks, walking track, bicycling, gym, putting green, volleyball, nearby tennis, massage, facials, full-service beauty salon, lectures, discussion groups, films, fashion shows, craft demonstrations.

Lodging

Accommodations are standard single, double or triple rooms, priced accordingly.

Cuisine

Several different diets are available depending upon an individual's weight loss goal and overall health. The spa nurse helps determine which diet is right for each guest. Daily calorie counts range from 700 to 1,000. Sometimes guests ask for more food; however, the spa policy is to not serve any individual more than 1,000 calories a day.

It's hard not to lose weight at the Bermuda Inn. Sample dishes from the menu include Cornish game hens, meat loaf, grilled halibut, crepes, lasagna and quiche.

WESTERN SPAS ■

Bermuda Inn Fitness
  and Reducing Resort
43019 Sierra Highway
Lancaster, CA 93534

805-942-1493
800-328-3276 (CA)
800-342-7546 (out of state)

CARMEL COUNTRY SPA

Carmel Valley, California

$$

Open: Year-round

The geography alone makes Carmel Country Spa worth visiting. Nestled in beautiful Carmel Valley, the spa is surrounded by rolling hills, oak trees and wildflowers. It's a half-hour from Big Sur, Monterey (with its Cannery Row, of John Steinbeck fame) and Carmel, a picture-perfect coastal town with a picture-perfect mayor, Clint Eastwood.

Location isn't the only thing going for Carmel Country Spa. There's the weather. The temperature usually ranges between 70 and 80 degrees, with low humidity.

The climate fosters ideal growing conditions for the spa's year-round vegetable and flower gardens. As a result, fresh produce and flowers are always in abundance.

The spa itself looks like a country club, minus a golf course. The rustic setting and wooden lodge epitomize western charm. This is California living at its best.

Most guests are women whose primary goal is to lose weight. (Physicians recommend the spa to diabetic or obese patients, although they don't represent the majority of guests.) Professional women and homemakers are represented in equal numbers.

The daily schedule of voluntary activities includes an 8 AM morning walk that is quite special, given the various settings: Carmel Beach, Garland Ranch, Quail Lodge, Pacific Grove, to name a few favorite spots.

Guests can consult privately with the staff to discuss the spa's diet program. Personalized diet and exercise regimens aren't available. Most guests lose a pound a day.

However, not everyone diets. Some people visit Carmel Country Spa simply to relax and get away from it all.

Activities & Services

Warm-up and stretch exercises, low-impact aerobics, aquacise, energizing and resistance exercises, yoga, health-related lectures, massage, salt rub, body wrap, facial, full-service beauty salon, walks, swimming, sauna, hot tub.

Lodging

Single, double and triple accommodations are available and priced accordingly. Rooms are like those of a standard hotel, equipped with telephones and televisions.

Cuisine

700 to 800 calories a day. Sample dishes include crab salad, baked fresh whole trout, spinach pie and Cornish game hen. The diet also includes eight glasses of water a day and various vitamin pills. Nondieters can eat as much of the diet food as they want.

Carmel Country Spa
10 Country Club Way
Carmel Valley, CA 93924   408-659-3486

LAKESIDE HEALTH RESORT

Lake Elsinore, California

$$$
Open: Year-round

California boasts some of the most sophisticated and expensive spas in the country — The Golden Door, Cal-a-Vie and Sonoma Mission Inn, to name a few. Lakeside Health Resort achieves the sophistication without the steep price.

Its program is as comprehensive and up-to-date as those featured at the super spas.

Lakeside's highly qualified managers and directors have a lot to do with the program's success. Their collective experience is impressive. General Manager Fay Antaky managed The Oaks at Ojai for nine years. Lakeside's program director, fitness and nutrition consultant, Judy Fabling, is a former staff member at The Golden Door and Rancho La Puerto, another first-rate spa. Lakeside's behavioral analyst, Kay Nelson, holds a Ph.D. in her field.

The Lakeside program is deeply rooted in behavior modification. It focuses on physical, nutritional, mental and emotional development and renewal of spirit—which usually happens automatically when everything else in life is running smoothly.

Weight loss is just one aspect of the multifaceted program. Guests learn the importance of exercise to reduce stress, improve energy, strengthen the cardiovascular and immune systems and, of course, keep their weight in check. They also examine new ways to think about food and how to break bad health habits.

Twice a day, experts lecture on topics ranging from "Cravings—Nutritional and Other Needs," "Self-Hypnosis, Aerobics and Fat Burning" to "Taking the Lakeside Program Home with You" and "Fit, Forty and Fabulous." Lectures are offered simultaneously with physical, nutritional, relaxation and beauty activities.

Lakeside offers so many classes and lectures that guests are advised on how to schedule everything during the first-day orientation.

Most guests are women, about half of whom are professionals and the other half, homemakers. The average age is 40, but senior citizens are also represented. Most guests aren't athletic. In fact, someone in tip-top shape would find Lakeside too easy.

About an hour southeast of Los Angeles, the resort is located on Lake Elsinore, a peaceful, rural setting in semi-arid high desert country.

■ AFFORDABLE SPAS

Activities & Services

Low-impact aerobics, "Better Backs & Bellies," stretch and walk, gentle stretch and tone (flexercise), aquacise, body conditioning, weight training, walks, back care exercises, yoga, massage, reflexology, herbal bath, body wrap. Full-service beauty salon (manicure, pedicure, hairstyling and more). Health-related lectures, swimming, bicycling, mountain hiking, hot tub, sauna, whirlpool, films.

Lodging

Recently remodeled single, double and triple rooms are available. The rooms, decorated in ocean blue, peach and mauve, face a central courtyard. The atmosphere is comfortable with a touch of country elegance.

Cuisine

700 to 900 calories a day. Sample dishes are stuffed trout with shrimp, Chinese vegetables and tostadas.

Lakeside Health Resort
32281 Riverside Drive
Lake Elsinore, CA 92330

714-674-1501
800-472-8583 (CA)

MEADOWLARK HEALTH AND GROWTH CENTER

Hemet, California

$$
Open: Year-round

This nonprofit holistic health retreat in Hemet, California, features an eclectic program, combining medicine, psychology, spirituality and the arts. Strenuous fitness isn't part of the routine; nor is weight loss a goal. Meadowlark's overall objective is to teach guests new ways to care for themselves and thereby improve their health.

The optional medically supervised fasting program isn't intended as a diet, but as a method of detoxifying the body, when combined with relaxation and meditation.

Adjacent to Meadowlark is the Holistic Medical Center, serving guests and Hemet residents. Its many services (offered to spa-goers a la carte) include acupuncture, homeopathic medicine, psychological and nutritional counseling, biofeedback and polarity massage.

Center activities change daily. A typical day might start with a biofeedback session at 9 AM, followed by swimming exercises, lunch and a siesta. At 2 PM, guests might take a yoga class, then a dream workshop.

The evening program can be anything from a holistic health lecture to a discussion about crystals and their healing powers.

Located on an estate built in 1914, Meadowlark was founded in 1957 by Dr. Evarts G. Loomis. Rolling green lawns, flower gardens, views of the towering San Jacinto Mountains and the ever-present sunshine (Hemet is famous for setting new temperature records) make Meadowlark a peaceful retreat.

The clientele runs the gamut from young professionals in their mid-twenties to senior citizens, from the physically fit to those wanting to shape up and improve their health.

Activities & Services

Stretch, release and balance, aquacise, parcourse, meditation, art workshops, dream workshops, biofeedback, yoga, polarity demonstrations, movement to music, cooking demonstrations, individual counseling, video presentations, expression in color. Lectures and group discussions with doctors, psychologists and other experts. Swimming, hot tub, bicycling.

Lodging

Some guest rooms are located in the original 1914 servants' quarters. For a slightly higher price, guests can

AFFORDABLE SPAS

stay in the estate's newer addition. The rooms aren't equipped with televisions or telephones, so guests can really get away from it all.

Cuisine

No diet plan is available. The health food menu includes standard offerings, such as stir-fry vegetables over rice and Mexican entrees. Supervised water and juice fasting programs are offered.

Meadowlark Health and Growth Center
26126 Fairview Avenue
Hemet, CA 92344   714-927-1343

MONACO VILLA RESORT HOTEL AND SPA

Palm Springs, California

$$
Open: October through June

It would be easy to mistake Monaco Villa for just another Palm Springs motel—a modern, white building with a parking lot in front and astro turf around the pool. However, it's one of the oldest and most respected weight loss spas in that region.

Monaco Villa more than lives up to its motto, "Lose a pound a day, the gourmet way." This is about as elegant as dieting can get. Dinner is served on fine china by candlelight. Typical low-calorie dishes include tornados of beef and chocolate mousse.

The diet program is designed not only for those who want to lose weight, but also for diabetics and individuals with cardiac conditions or high blood pressure.

Monaco Villa attracts the type of patron who dominated the ranks of spa-goers until recently—homemakers with grown children. However, younger

WESTERN SPAS

women are also well represented these days, according to spa owner Anne Cobin. And men are more than welcome. The spa is particularly popular with men and women who want to lose weight but can't stomach the spartan, vegetarian cuisine often served at weight loss spas.

Monaco Villa offers a supervised physical fitness program of voluntary activities, ranging from aerobics to pool exercises. Upon arrival, guests consult individually with the staff to determine specific needs and goals.

The spa has only eight guest rooms. Thus, the classes are small, and personal attention is guaranteed.

Activities & Services

Calisthenics, aerobics, aquacise, swimming, hot jet therapy pool, yoga, massage, health and nutrition discussions. Nearby golf, tennis and horseback riding.

Lodging

The homey guest rooms offer spa-goers a relaxing, peaceful atmosphere.

Cuisine

For women, 500 to 750 calories a day; for men, 750 to 900 calories. Sample dishes are veal picatta, shrimp scampi, crepe Florentine, orange lemon chiffon whip and baked Alaska. High-protein cuisine is available for nondieters.

Monaco Villa Resort Hotel and Spa
371 Camino Monte Vista
Palm Springs, CA 92262   619-327-1261

■ AFFORDABLE SPAS

MURRIETA HOT SPRINGS RESORT, SPA AND CONFERENCE CENTER

$$

Murrieta, California   Open: Year-round

This European-style spa is famous for its mud baths and Mediterranean architecture, reminiscent of Hearst Castle. Surrounded by green lawns, palm trees and golden hills, the spa looms like an oasis in the California desert.

Located 90 minutes southeast of Los Angeles, Murrieta was once owned and operated by the Murrieta Foundation, a nonprofit educational organization. The foundation restored and renovated many of the spa's historic buildings, such as the 1904 assembly hall, the 1926 mud bath building and the 1906 Monterey Hotel building.

People of all ages come to Murrieta for a variety of reasons: to "take the waters," relieve arthritis, get away from it all, get more in touch with their feelings and get in shape.

Based on the best of European and American spa traditions, Murrieta's spa programs feature mud baths, mineral waters and herbal wraps, combined with a holistic regimen that includes vegetarian diet cuisine, exercise and self-awareness workshops.

A number of unique spa packages, not all of them diet- or fitness-related, are available. Some weekend programs include "Personal Insights" (how to gain new perspectives in problem solving) and "Polarity Bodywork" (how to relax and release tension). Some week-long programs include "Fit 'n' Trim" (for weight loss and toning), "Stress Management" (understanding the mental and physical origins of stress) and "Dynamic Relationships" (how to get more satisfaction and closeness from a relationship).

The spa also offers mini-day packages, such as the "Hot Springs Special," which includes an energy balancing body session, mineral bath with essential oils and an aromatic body wrap.

Guests can select classes and services on an a la carte basis and create their own special program. Children are more than welcome. Although Murrieta doesn't have programs especially for them, children can participate in some of the adult classes and activities.

Murrieta offers a variety of baths, wraps, body work and natural skincare therapies. No one should miss the mud bath. The mud works like a poultice, softening the skin. Mixed in with the mud are peat moss, which holds in the warmth, and sea kelp, which increases the mineral content.

A ten-minute dip into that heavy, warm miracle mixture is an exotic experience. At first, it's a strange sensation, but most guests like it after a minute. An attendant helps mud-laden guests climb out of the tub and hoses them off. That's followed by a ten-minute soak in a tub filled with hot mineral spring water. Then, it's off to the wrapping tables, where guests swaddled in white sheets lie on tables for 20 minutes. The results are soft, clean skin and mellow guests.

Activities & Services

Aquacise, exercise classes, aromatic body wrap, nature care wrap (34 herbs massaged on hands, face and feet), mud bath, essential oil mineral bath, energy balancing session (a massage to relieve tense, tight areas), Swedish massage, face and scalp massage, salt glow rub, lymph massage, facial, back facial, foot care, awareness counseling, workshops on subjects such as "Vegetarian Cooking" and "Health-Building Friendships," lectures on natural skincare and other health-related topics, natural mineral pools, swimming, tennis, films, dinner theater.

Lodging

Guests can choose a large, modern room in the Lodge, a quaint cottage with a wonderful view or a room in the older part of the spa with California oak furnishings.

Cuisine

Murrieta's Oasis Restaurant is the largest vegetarian restaurant in the U.S. It's been known to serve over 1,000 pounds of tofu a day! Guests who want to diet can consult

AFFORDABLE SPAS

with the staff, who will prescribe a diet plan consisting of certain proportions of the regularly served vegetarian cuisine. A sampling from the hearty, healthy menu is vegetable souffle, homemade pasta, jam and whole wheat bread, tofu casserole, tempura and apple crisp.

Murrieta Hot Springs Resort,
   Spa and Conference Center   714-677-7451
39405 Murrieta Hot Springs Road   800-458-4393 (CA)
Murrieta, CA 92362   800-322-4542 (out of state)

THE OAKS AT OJAI

Ojai, California $ and $$
      Year-round

    This reputable California spa gets glowing reports from guests, who rave about its professional programs, lovely setting and price (approximately $100 a day, double occupancy, including three meals and most activities).
    Owned and operated by physical fitness specialist Sheila Cluff—who also owns The Palms at Palm Springs—the spa is located in Ojai, a charming art colony 80 minutes north of Los Angeles. Because The Oaks is right in the middle of Ojai, guests can easily visit the town's attractive shops. A park adjacent to the spa is the site of well-known music and folk dance festivals.
    But what really makes Ojai so popular is the beautiful countryside—soft, rolling hills covered with golden grass and majestic old oak trees.
    The Oaks offers 18 daily fitness classes at beginning through advanced levels. Classes are optional. However, it's recommended that each guest participate in at least one daily stretch class, aerobics activity and muscle strengthening class per day for maximum benefits. The classes (listed below) are often creative and fun—for example, "Body Awareness," "Creative Aerobics" and "Fitness Potpourri"

(techniques for relaxation and stress reduction, self-massage, fitness and nutrition lectures).

In addition to classes, The Oaks offers lectures, beauty treatments, massage and a multitude of outdoor recreational activities, such as golf and horseback riding at a nearby stable.

Counseling with a registered nurse or an exercise physiologist is also available. Because the spa's three meals and two snacks a day add up to a only 750 calories, guests lose weight at The Oaks.

A number of special packages are available, including the popular "Spa Day," a terrific bargain. For $60 a day, guest receive three low-calorie gourmet meals, locker room facilities, plus access to all spa facilities and exercise classes, evening lectures and craft classes. (Massages and facials cost extra.) Other specials, which change all the time, include "Art Appreciation Weekend," "Spa Cuisine Cooking Week" (featuring demonstrations by well-known chefs and cookbook authors) and "Hiking and Jogging Week."

The spa attracts professional women, including actresses from Los Angeles who find the unpretentious surroundings and casual atmosphere relaxing. The Oaks' guest list also includes some men.

Activities & Services

Aerobics, body awareness, creative aerobics, body dynamics (for advanced guests), aquacise, weight training, body contouring, yoga, ultrasound body awareness (a six-page computerized print-out, explaining an individual's body muscle and fat content), evening lectures, massage, facials, makeup design, wardrobe consultation, full-service beauty salon, walks, swimming.

Lodging

Guest bungalows, nestled beneath shady oak trees, offer simple and comfortable accommodations, with the three important basics: private bath, color television and air conditioning.

■ AFFORDABLE SPAS

Cuisine

750 calories a day. Sample dishes are tostadas, ravioli, lasagne, spaghetti, fish and chicken.

The Oaks at Ojai
122 E. Ojai Avenue
Ojai, CA 93023   805-646-5573

THE PALMS AT PALM SPRINGS

Palm Springs, California

$ and $$
Open: Year-round

Sheila Cluff, owner of this excellent Palm Springs spa, also owns the well-regarded Oaks at Ojai spa. A former professional figure skater, phys. ed. teacher and model, Cluff is the author of *Aerobic Body Contouring* and a frequent talk show guest. She also owns Fitness Inc. and Fit II, enterprises specializing in fitness, wellness, fashion and beauty seminars.

Needless to say, Cluff is on the cutting edge of the health, fitness and diet movement. And her spa programs show it.

The spa offers 16 voluntary fitness classes a day. The staff recommends that guests participate in at least one stretch, one aerobic and one strength training class daily. The theory is that combining the three promotes maximum results. Some classes are targeted at different fitness levels. Private fitness consultations and body composition analysis sessions are offered by appointment only.

The "Introduction to Fitness" class is recommended for the first day. It helps update guests' fitness information and gives them guidelines for selecting classes. Fortunately, most exercise classes can be continued at home.

The Palms offers a number of special summer packages. "Mother/Daughter Days" includes a 50 percent discount for a daughter sharing a room with her mom. "Friendship Day" makes the sociable gesture of a 25 percent discount for a double room shared by two friends. The "His and Hers" special allows couples to spend half of their stay at the spa for free. Other packages include "Women's Business and Professional Networking Week," "Cuisine Cooking Week" and "Fitness Networking Week."

For spa-goers with wanderlust, Cluff also leads special health and fitness tours (usually via cruise ships) to spas in different parts of the world.

Located in a lovely renovated Mediterranean manor house with rugged mountains in the background, The Palms is within walking distance of Palm Springs' fashionable shops and restaurants. (The restaurants are tempting, but most people stick to the Palms' diet plan.)

The spa mostly attracts women, about half of whom are professionals seeking stress relief. Homemakers are also represented. Most guests visit The Palms to lose weight and get in shape. However, guests at the spa usually aren't noticeably overweight. A few want to shed 20 pounds or more, but most are battling five to ten pounds.

Activities & Services

Body awareness, toning and stretching, creative aerobics, orientation to fitness, body dynamics (advanced aerobics), aquacise, body shaping and strength training (weight training), body conditioning (light weights and rubber bands), aerobic body conditioning (low-impact aerobic movements and light wrist weights), yoga, massage, facials, full-service beauty salon, color analysis, makeup lessons, swimming, whirlpool, gym, sauna, nature walks, celebrity walks (to view stars' homes). Nearby tennis, golf, hot-air ballooning, bicycling and horseback riding.

Lodging

Guest rooms are simple and unpretentious. (The Palms prides itself on having a first-rate spa program, not

AFFORDABLE SPAS

on luxury accommodations.) Guests share rooms, unless they specifically request a private room.

Cuisine

750 to 1,000 calories a day or "athletes' portions" (50 percent more) of the diet food for nondieters. Sample dishes are lasagna, crepes, cheesecake, homemade soup and tostadas.

The Palms at Palm Springs
572 North Indian Avenue
Palm Springs, CA 92262   619-325-1111

PALM SPRINGS SPA HOTEL AND MINERAL SPRINGS

Palm Springs, California $, $$ and $$$
                                  Open: Year-round

Six hundred years ago, Cahuilla Indians came to these mineral springs to take the waters. Today, they're the site of the Palm Springs Spa Hotel, and people come for the same reason—and to shape up.

Most spas with natural mineral springs are more rustic than luxurious. However, this exceptional spa is a first-rate hotel with a top-notch health program but without the usual spa restrictions on alcohol or coffee.

An impressive staff of professional dieticians, therapists, aerobics instructors, masseurs, facialists and beauticians supervise the "Spaerobics" program, which includes aerobics and aquacise, low-calorie cuisine, and diet and health consultations.

Guests are offered a variety of morning exercise classes and afternoon beauty and relaxation services. They can create their own itinerary or ask the staff for assistance. Computerized fitness evaluations are available for an additional fee.

Individual mineral whirlpool baths and two outdoor mineral pools are available for guest use. As a special touch, after a hot mineral bath, guests are encouraged to lie down on a small bed in one of the quiet cooling rooms where an attendant serves them herbal tea or ice water. Hair dryers, robes, shampoo and towels are provided in the spa's dressing rooms.

The pace here is very low-key and casual. There is no pressure to lose weight or be the best at aerobics. Most guests are more concerned with improving their overall health via light exercise, stress reduction and low-calorie food, versus rigid dieting and workouts.

The spa attracts a mix of people, including celebrities, senior citizens and homemakers. Recently the spa program and facilities were redesigned to attract young professionals, too. Most guests are women between the ages of 30 and 50.

The Palm Springs Spa Hotel, decorated in taupe, purple and pink desert colors, is located in central Palm Springs, close to its famous specialty shops and restaurants. The San Jacinto Mountains serve as a dramatic backdrop for the hotel and spa.

Activities & Services

Stretching exercises in mineral springs or pool, whirlpool baths, mineral baths, aerobics, gym with Lifecycles, life rower, free weights. Eucalyptus inhalation room, cooling rooms, Swedish and Orthion massage, shoulder and neck massage, facial, makeup analysis, manicure, pedicure, solarium, swimming, tennis.

Lodging

All rooms are decorated in muted sandy desert colors. Some have balconies with views. All have refrigerators.

AFFORDABLE SPAS

Cuisine

1,000 calories a day. All diet and nondiet meals are served in Rennick's restaurant in the hotel. This is California spa cuisine at its fresh and imaginative best: cold salmon, medallions of lamb, scallops with whole wheat pasta, shrimp and vegetables grilled with dill, papaya and yogurt with fresh fruit.

Palm Springs Spa Hotel
  and Mineral Springs   619-325-1461
100 North Indian Avenue   800-472-4371 (CA)
Palm Springs, CA 92262   800-854-1279 (out of state)

WEIGHT WATCHERS AT THE SURFSIDE INN
$$

Santa Barbara, California   Open: Year-round

Santa Barbara fulfills everyone's fantasy of California — classic Spanish architecture, the Pacific Ocean on one side, the Santa Inez Mountains on the other, groves of olive and orange trees, birds of paradise.

In addition, it boasts a thriving cultural community: art galleries, arts and crafts shows, the botanical gardens, polo matches, historic El Paseo with its quaint shops, whale watching, horseback riding, historic missions, magnificent beaches, boating and fishing.

Those who can tear themselves away from all those temptations long enough to check into the Weight Watchers program at The Surfside Inn are in good hands. When it comes to dieting, this group knows what works.

Throughout the day, guests are offered a choice of exercise classes, motivational workshops, and relaxation and beauty treatments. The exercise classes aren't difficult. Although guests can participate in as many or as few classes as they like, the staff recommends that everyone take a minimum of two classes a day.

The staff is extremely enthusiastic and supportive. Most of them were once overweight. Upon request, they'll develop an exercise regimen based on a guest's personal goals and lifestyle.

Weight Watchers' workshops teach guests how to plan menus and prepare food when the spa vacation is over, how to handle difficult diet situations (such as dining out and entertaining), how to control stress, keep weight loss motivation high and assert oneself.

Activities & Services

Aerobics, aquacise, stretch and tone (flexercise), yoga, walks, workshops, lectures, behavior modification classes, personal exercise program, nutritional counseling, group support sessions, massage, herbal body wrap, loofah body polish, facials, hand and foot massage, manicure, pedicure, makeup application lesson, swimming, golf, tennis.

Lodging

Guest rooms are clean and nicely appointed. (Try to reserve one with a view of the mountains.)

Cuisine

1,000 calories a day. Sample dishes are poached salmon with sauce verte, sweet potato vichyssoise, red snapper with sesame vegetables and honeyed pumpkin custard.

Surfside Inn
1111 East Cabrillo Boulevard
Santa Barbara, CA 93103

For more information on this and other Weight Watchers' spa programs, contact

Weight Watchers Resorts and Spas 313-443-1414
15815 W. 12 Mile Road 800-LEANER-U
Southfield, MI 48076 800-826-5088 (Canada)

■ AFFORDABLE SPAS

WILBUR HOT SPRINGS HEALTH SANCTUARY
$
Williams, California   **Open: Year-round**

Wilbur Hot Springs is similar in many ways to a European spa. It doesn't have a fitness program and no one's on a diet. The focus is on massage, relaxation and soaking in silky, therapeutic hot springs — just like at most European spas.

Guests visiting Wilbur Hot Springs Health Sanctuary for the first time feel as if they've stepped back in time to the wild West. The rugged California landscape looks like something out of "The Lone Ranger": deep canyons, valleys, gorges and granite walls, digger pines, scrub oaks, manzanitas and chaparral.

The Victorian-style health sanctuary looks just like it did during the Gold Rush, when it was a hotel on a stagecoach line. It's untouched by such modern conveniences as electricity. Evenings are illuminated by kerosene lamps, and heat is provided by a wood burning stove.

The massage program is comprehensive and the masseuses and masseurs are excellent. Twice a year Wilbur offers a two-week, 100-hour massage certification program.

The bathhouse features three spring-fed baths, ranging in temperature from 98 to 110 degrees. A large outdoor spring-fed mineral bath is kept warm in winter, cool in summer. Coed soaking in the buff is commonplace. In between dunks, guests sunbathe on the redwood deck, practice yoga, hike, meditate or get a massage.

Wilbur is also an artists' colony. Its artist-in-residence program attracts writers, poets, musicians and artists who work 20 hours a week in exchange for room, board, use of the facilities and an idyllic environment in which to be creative. It's not unusual to wander through the hotel and hear someone playing Vivaldi on a flute.

WESTERN SPAS

Activities & Services

Swedish, deep tissue, shiatsu, Trager and other forms of massage. Yoga, T'ai Chi, hiking, guided nature walks, spring-water swimming, geothermal tubs, dunk tub, volleyball, music room, billiards.

Lodging

Rooms in the hotel can accommodate two to four guests. They're decorated in understated, rustic hues reflecting turn-of-the-century western style. An 18-bed group room is also available.

Cuisine

BYO is the plan at Wilbur. All guests supply their own food and prepare it in the large, well-equipped hotel kitchen. Wine and beer are allowed in moderation in the dining room.

Wilbur Hot Springs Health Sanctuary
Star Route
Williams, CA 95987   916-473-2306

ZANE HAVEN

Palm Springs, California

$ and $$
Open: Year-round

Anyone interested in developing his or her biceps, triceps and quadriceps will be in heaven at Zane Haven. It's owned and operated by Christine Zane and her husband, Frank, who has won every bodybuilding title imaginable: Mr. America, Mr. World, Mr. Universe and Mr. Olympia.

The Zanes are not just muscle-builders but are also the authors of three fitness books — *The Zane Way to a Beautiful Body*, *Super Bodies in 12 Weeks* and *Zane Nutrition*.

AFFORDABLE SPAS

Not all of Zane Haven's guests are seasoned bodybuilders, nor is everyone young and muscular. The average age is 40, and beginning bodybuilders far outnumber pros. Most guests are professionals in fairly good physical condition who want to start a bodybuilding program.

The Zane program, which limits classes to eight people maximum, includes weight training, stretching, ab-aerobics (difficult stomach exercises), deep relaxation, nutritional counseling and motivational techniques.

Dieting is not a part of the program. Meals aren't even served. Everyone dines at local restaurants. However, nutrition is an integral part of the bodybuilding program. Guests are asked to keep a daily journal of everything they eat in order to become aware of nutritional habits, good and bad.

The Zanes teach guests how to select the right balance of protein, fat and carbohydrates to keep body fat at a minimum and muscle tone at a maximum.

Zane Haven offers one-day introductory programs with only two people per class, and a four- or five-day "Body Transformation Vacation" package. That program includes a combination of weight training sessions, seminars on everything from nutrition to stress management, a variety of relaxation techniques and resort-like activities such as swimming and sunbathing.

Frank Zane personally teaches each guest correct weight training exercises for all parts of the body. Beginners are taught how to lose excess fat, strengthen muscles, become aerobically fit and tighten their waistlines.

Professional bodybuilders are given posing and training tips for winning competitions. All guests are ensured a lot of individualized attention.

Participation in all classes and activities is mandatory. One woman who came with her son thought she'd get to spend a week relaxing by the pool while her son developed his biceps. But the Zanes had other ideas. After much moaning and groaning, she got into the spirit of things. By the end of the week, she had developed her own waist-reducing program and was elated with the results.

Zane Haven feels like a small lodge. There are only four guest rooms. It's located within walking distance of Palm Springs' numerous shops and restaurants.

Activities & Services

Workout organization seminars, weight training, ab-aerobics, stretching, flotation tank. Gym with free weights, Soloflex, Nautilus equipment, rowing machines. Stress management, guided deep relaxation, visualization techniques (to keep motivation up), affirmation, meditation, self-hypnosis, nutrition classes, Jacuzzi, swimming.

Lodging

Simple guest rooms are furnished with two beds and no television or radio.

Cuisine

Because kitchen facilities are not available, guests patronize Palm Springs' many restaurants.

Zane Haven 619-323-7486
P.O. Box 2031 800-548-4434 (CA)
Palm Springs, CA 92263 800-323-7537 (out of state)

COLORADO

THE ASPEN CLUB

Aspen, Colorado

$$$/Summer and Fall
Open: Year-round

Although many spas offer personalized diet and fitness programs, few compare with The Aspen Club's. That's not surprising, given the spa's affiliation with The Aspen Club Fitness and Sports Medicine Institute, which specializes in the prevention of sports injuries. In fact, spa participants

AFFORDABLE SPAS

can take advantage of the institute's highly sophisticated evaluation center.

Upon arrival, guests are evaluated and tested by a physician, physical therapist and various trainers. Every health and fitness test imaginable is administered: stress test with electrocardiogram readings, pulmonary function test, body fat measurements, strength and flexibility measurements, blood chemistry and more. In addition, a guest's eating habits are assessed.

After the tests are completed, guests are given an exercise prescription and their own trainer to help them implement the highly structured, individualized program.

"If you're a traveling salesman who spends a lot of time in motels, we're not going to tell you that you need to ride a stationary bicycle for 45 minutes every day when you're hardly ever near one," says The Aspen Club Vice President R. J. Gallagher. "We'll create a program that's realistic and fits in with your lifestyle. If you eat out a lot in restaurants, we'll teach you how to read the menu and what to order to keep your weight down."

A typical day at the spa might include an early morning walk through groves of aspen trees, breakfast in The Aspen Club, followed by a slow stretch class and aerobics. Afternoon activities might include a workout on Nautilus equipment, a seminar on nutrition, fitness or health, and a massage or facial.

The spa program is popular with athletes, as well as men and women who've never exercised. Because it's located in the country's most luxurious ski resort area, the spa tends to attract an affluent clientele that includes everyone from homemakers to executives (including the CEO of Pillsbury).

The sophisticated fitness program isn't designed for fast weight loss. In fact, during a week-long stay, guests have been known to gain a pound or two in muscle—not fat. "You may not lose a pound here," comments Gallagher. "But you'll be 20 times as fit as when you arrived."

The spa is ideal for people who don't necessarily have a weight problem, but want to become firmer, stronger and

WESTERN SPAS

healthier. It features various programs, including a three- and five-day "Health Evaluation Program" and a three- and five-day "Slimming and Firming Program." Children's programs are available.

(The Aspen Club operates year-round. However, winter and spring prices are considerably higher than the "affordable" pricing standards used in this book.)

Activities & Services

Low-impact aerobics, aikido (a form of martial arts), slow stretch, aquacise, ski conditioning, video stroke analysis (a videotape and analysis of a guest exercising), water volleyball, scuba diving, swimming, Nautilus equipment, free-weight clinics, personal training, basketball, wallyball (volleyball played off a wall instead of a net), squash, tennis, racquetball clinics, walks, volleyball, cycling, triathlon, cardiovascular training, fitness evaluation (described above), massage, facials, sauna, Jacuzzi, steam bath, seminars and lectures.

Lodging

Spa-goers stay in The Aspen Club Lodge, a first-rate hotel with every amenity imaginable—from airport limousine service and a full-service concierge to beautiful baths stocked with toiletries.

Cuisine

Guests never get bored with the diet. Low-calorie cuisine is served in The Aspen Club (no set daily calorie count), but guests also can dine in some of Aspen's finest restaurants, which specially prepare low-calorie dishes for spa guests.

The Aspen Club
1450 Crystal Lake Road
Aspen, CO 81611

303-925-6760
800-443-2582 (CO)
800-882-2582 (out of state)

151

■ AFFORDABLE SPAS

MOUNTAIN MEADOWS CENTER

$

Jamestown, Colorado   Open: Year-round

If all you do at this cozy health retreat is sit on the deck and admire the view, it won't be the first time a spa-goer has been distracted by the magnificent scenery. This Colorado spa overlooks the Roosevelt National Forest and the nearby Continental Divide.

Mountain Meadows' accommodations are simple, the rates very reasonable (about $75 a day per person, including meals and most activities) and the ambience relaxed, casual and friendly.

The holistic-based program revolves around light exercise (the altitude makes strenuous workouts difficult, if not dangerous), relaxation, getting in touch with nature and self-renewal.

Mountain Meadows can only accommodate ten guests at a time, so personal attention is guaranteed. Most guests are professional women between the ages of 25 and 45.

Some activities vary with the season (e.g., cross-country skiing and hiking). Other activities and services, such as exercise classes, massage and yoga, are offered year-round. The center usually doesn't plan evening activities. However, many guests like to drive to the University of Colorado in nearby Boulder to attend a lecture.

During the winter, guests spend a lot of time in front of the fireplace talking the night away. The outdoor hot tub provides relaxation under the stars year-round.

Activities & Services

Aerobics, hiking, cross-country skiing, yoga, gym with free weights and other conditioning equipment, massage, facials, hot tub, psychic demonstrations and lectures that address guests' interests.

Lodging

The chalet-style lodge includes five guest bedrooms, all with twin beds, shared baths and views. Guests can sunbathe on a large deck overlooking the mountains.

Cuisine

The 1,000- to 1,300-calorie-a-day menu includes dishes such as Rocky Mountain trout, fresh garden salads, bran muffins and poppy seed cakes. Alcohol isn't available. However, guests frequently bring wine.

Mountain Meadows Center
P.O. Box 205
Jamestown, CO 80455   303-939-9887

ROCKY MOUNTAIN WELLNESS SPA

Steamboat Springs, Colorado

$$$/April to November
Open: Year-round

Steamboat Springs could make a nature lover out of even the most stalwart city slicker. Just looking at the snow-capped mountains, sweeping panoramic views, meadowlands bursting with wildflowers and pine forest makes you feel healthy.

The spa offers a computer-assisted "wellness" program based on reducing stress, increasing energy and promoting physical and emotional well-being.

Before arriving, guests complete a nutrition questionnaire to determine vitamin and mineral deficiencies and excesses. When they arrive, guests discuss personal goals with the spa staff. A registered nurse evaluates each person's cardiovascular system, metabolism, body fat content and toxic levels. All that information enables the staff to design a "life-

AFFORDABLE SPAS

style health plan" for each guest. The plan includes a nutrition program, exercises and stress-reduction techniques.

A typical day at the spa might include deep-stretching, stress-releasing exercises and a walk, followed by individual stress evaluations and exercise instruction. After lunch, many guests take another walk on trails near the lodge. The rest of the afternoon might include a trip to a nearby hot mineral springs for a therapeutic soak, a brief walk to a spectacular waterfall, a game of tennis, swimming, cross-country skiing in the winter and a sauna or massage.

Many guests spend the afternoon practicing the stress-reducing exercises and techniques they learned that morning. At night, they often take a quiet walk under the stars.

After dinner, private and group seminars are offered on subjects such as nutrition, stress reduction, self-celebration (confidence building), love and relationships, communicating, forgiveness and thankfulness, and peak performance (exercises and mental training to help reach a performance level far beyond one's expectations — popular with professional athletes and corporate executives).

Guests can skip the seminars and browse through the spa's library. You won't find Danielle Steele or Robert Ludlum novels on the shelves, but rather a collection of books on health, nutrition, fitness and other topics related to the spa's programs.

Rocky Mountain Wellness Spa is a good bet for anyone suffering from job burnout. In fact, more people come to the spa for stress reduction than weight loss. Although the latter is of concern to many, this isn't the type of spa that attracts people who want to shed pounds and indulge in a multitude of beauty treatments. Instead, the emphasis is on long-term behavior modification. To monitor guests' progress with stress reduction, the spa staff does follow-up calls to spa-goers for up to six months after their stay.

A little more than half the guests are women; the age span is approximately 30 to 50.

From April to November, the off-season rates are approximately $1,075 for a six-night stay (double occupancy, including all meals, taxes, tips and most services). During ski season, the program is more expensive.

Activities & Services

Personally instructed stress-reduction techniques and exercises, wellness evaluation, nutritional counseling, private consultations, mineral and vitamin analysis, wellness seminars and lectures, massage, sauna, hiking, tennis, bicycling, pool swimming, exercise gym, field trips, cross-country skiing, downhill skiing and instruction, ice skating, facials, manicures, pedicures, tennis instruction, golf and instruction, hot-air ballooning, horseback riding, sailing, windsurfing, swimming instruction, rafting. Programs addressing smoking, cholesterol and management training.

Lodging

Modern chalet-style accommodations with double or single rooms and private bath are available. Two guests can share a suite with a living room, fireplace, balcony and views.

Cuisine

A 900- to 1,200-calorie allergy-free diet is served. Sample dishes are stuffed artichokes, oatbran muffins, fresh fruit and yogurt, New Zealand white fish with dill sauce, guacamole dip and fruit frappe.

Rocky Mountain Wellness Spa
Box 777
Steamboat Springs, CO 80477

303-879-7772
800-345-7770

■ AFFORDABLE SPAS

VAIL HOTEL AND ATHLETIC CLUB

Vail, Colorado

$$$/Summer
Open: Year-round

Although the winter prices at the luxurious Vail Hotel are steep, summer is a different story. When the snow melts and the skiers pack up their gear and head home, the hotel cuts its rates almost by half, making this super fitness retreat a good bargain.

The summer temperature — 65 to 80 degrees — is so mild that air conditioning isn't necessary. And there aren't even the usual bugs of summer. The Colorado sky is vivid blue and the mountain meadows are blanketed with beautiful alpine flowers.

The club and spa offer daily aerobics classes in addition to services such as massage and Nautilus. Some classes are for beginners; others for those more advanced. There also are plenty of outdoor activities, such as golf, tennis, river rafting and gondola rides.

The hotel is located in the heart of Vail, an Austrian-style village with chalets and window boxes. Free bus service is provided throughout the village, so guests don't have to bother with a car. (Vail is home to 150 European-style boutiques, 80 restaurants and lounges.)

The athletic club is located in the hotel and is available for no extra cost to all guests. Local residents are also club members. Generally, Vail residents can be summed up in two words: young and athletic.

Activities & Services

Aerobics, Nautilus equipment, free-weight room, Swedish and shiatsu massage, fitness analysis, stretch, yoga, aquacise, eucalyptus steam room, solarium, sauna, whirlpool, outdoor hot tub, hydrotherapy pool, racquetball, squash, swimming, full-service beauty salon. Nearby activities: hiking, bicycling, golf, horseback riding, fishing, white-water rafting, boating, mountain climbing.

Lodging

Tastefully decorated guest rooms range from doubles to penthouse suites. Most rooms have balconies and views of Vail Mountain.

Cuisine

Although diet cuisine isn't available, Vail is a gourmet heaven. The Vail Athletic Club specializes in California cuisine. Popular dishes include grilled swordfish with orange ginger sauce, blackened salmon, roast duck with peach sauce and vegetable platters.

Vail Hotel and Athletic Club   303-476-0700
352 East Meadow Drive   800-626-4144 (CO)
Vail, CO 81657   800-822-4754 (out of state)

HAWAII

KALANI HONUA INTERCULTURAL RETREAT AND CONFERENCE CENTER

$

Kalapana Beach, Hawaii   **Open: Year-round**

This holistic retreat is the ultimate health vacation. As far as accommodations go, it's definitely no frills. But who needs room service and cable television in paradise?

Located on the Big Island of Hawaii (Honolulu is on more densely populated Oahu), Kalani is surrounded by ocean on one side and tropical forest on the other.

This is the Hawaii one dreams about — no high-rise hotels or busloads of tourists. Consider some of the sightseeing available within a ten-mile radius of the resort: five national parks (including the spectacular Hawaii Volcanoes), Kaimu and Kehena black sand beaches, the ancient temple of Wahaula, Waiwelawela hot springs, Chain of Craters steam baths, King's ceremonial trail, snorkeling, tide pools, Crater Lake, two historic churches, the village of Pahoa and orchid farms.

Surrounded by all those tropical temptations, who has time for aerobics? Although some guests spend a lot of time pursuing activities outside the spa, the crowd at Kalani is health-conscious, and participation in its various programs is high. Most guests are young or middle-aged and in good physical condition. Says Director Richard Koob, "We're not designed to facilitate people of marginal health, in fact, most of our guests are robust, adventuresome and healthy."

Weight loss isn't of major concern to most guests, although low-calorie cuisine is served and consultants can supervise and design an exercise/weight loss program.

Serving an equal number of men and women, Kalani is popular with families, couples and singles. However, most guests are conference group participants, wanting select programs tailored to their needs and interests.

Throughout the year, different holistic health and spiritual workshops (e.g., a yoga retreat) are offered, in addition to visual arts seminars, language programs, dance programs and an annual performing arts festival.

Activities & Services

Yoga, aerobics, sports conditioning, massage (Swedish, shiatsu and acupressure), hot tub, Jacuzzi, sauna. Warm springs. Oceanfront bicycling, swimming, tennis, hiking, snorkeling, scuba diving, volleyball. Evening dance parties, hulas and Hawaiian cultural events.

Lodging

Hexagonal cedar lodges with private or shared baths and kitchens are available for individuals, couples or families. For those who want to sleep in the Hawaiian moonlight, campsites are also available.

Cuisine

Dieting Hawaiian-style is a treat. Sample dishes from the low-calorie menu (no set daily calorie count) include papaya-passion fruit and banana smoothies. The popular breakfast buffet offers tropical fruits (pineapple, of course), yogurt, brown rice and French toast. Nondiet dishes include baked mushroom, lemon and garlic mahi-mahi, spinach lasagna, cream of curried papaya cashew soup, sauteed vegetables with tempeh and tahini sauce. Beer and wine are available.

Kalani Honua Intercultural Retreat
   and Conference Center
Box 4500
Kalapana Beach, HI 96778   808-965-7828

IDAHO

BREAK AWAY TOTAL HEALTH AND FITNESS RESORT

$$$

Sandpoint, Idaho   **Open: Spring, Fall, Winter**

Break Away Total Health and Fitness Resort in Idaho's lake and mountain country is a haven for vacationers who want to mix structured fitness activities with recreational sports. Winter spa-goers can take advantage of the area's ski slopes; spring and fall visitors can fish, water ski and sail. (The Break Away health and fitness program isn't offered in the summer.)

Break Away is housed in the Edgewater Resort, an unpretentious motor inn located along the shores of Lake Pend Oreille. Despite its rustic setting, the program is as comprehensive and professional as that of a super spa.

Upon arrival, guests receive an orientation and a fitness evaluation, which includes a computerized read-out of body

159

fat percentage, base metabolism and point of dehydration. A nutritionist helps guests develop a diet plan.

The health and fitness program offers a variety of activities from which to choose. A typical day might include a 7 AM walk, a personal fitness evaluation, a choice between aerobics, yoga, stretch and tone (flexercise) or recreational sports, a guided hike or bicycle tour, massage or herbal wrap, personal counseling, swimming, health-related group discussions and/or workshops.

Many activities are held in the Sandpoint West Athletic Club, a short drive from the Edgewater. (Guests should plan their day carefully, or they could spend a lot of time going back and forth between the Edgewater and the Club.)

For evening entertainment, guests sometimes attend a local theater or walk to a nearby Italian restaurant, which serves a specially prepared low-calorie meal.

Break Away also offers a number of special packages, such as "Fitness Appreciation Week," "Entrepreneur Week," "Couples Week" and "Family Week." Those packages include some of the activities described above, in addition to seminars, workshops and classes of particular relevance to each group.

The town of Sandpoint is something of a throwback to the sixties. Many residents are middle-aged hippies who relocated to this bucolic setting more than 20 years ago. Until recently, about half of the town residents shunned tourism, but that's started to change. The area's shopping is very unique, featuring a lot of locally made crafts.

In contrast to the town's population, Break Away attracts a lot of professionals from Washington (the closest major airport is Spokane), California and Canada. Most guests focus on stress reduction. The ratio of men to women is about 3:7; the median age, 30 to 35.

Activities & Services

Yoga, low-impact aerobics, stretch and tone (flexercise), aquacise, weight training, body composition analysis, hikes, jogging, nutritional planning, individual counseling, sauna, Jacuzzi, tanning room, massage, allergy testing, manicure, pedicure, facial. Seminars and lectures on stress management, goal-setting, communication, time management, eating disorders, assertiveness training. Recreational activities — skiing (half-day lift ticket included in package price), cross-country skiing, racquetball, bicycling, swimming, golf, squash, water skiing, mountain climbing, canoeing, windsurfing, fishing and shopping.

Lodging

Accommodations are like those of any clean, well-managed motor inn, complete with phone, color TV and room service. Most rooms have twin beds. Every room faces either the lake or the picturesque Cabinet Mountains.

Cuisine

A 1,400-calorie diet is served. Popular dishes include eggs Benedict, shrimp salad, baked cod and crab, homemade muffins and fresh strawberries. Meals are served in the Edgewater dining room, which also serves nondiet food. Alcohol is available, although not recommended for guests interested in losing weight.

Break Away Total Health and Fitness Resort
P.O. Box 1868   208-263-3194
Sandpoint, ID 83864   800-635-2534 (out of state)

NEVADA

MGM DESERT INN HOTEL AND CASINO
$$
Las Vegas, Nevada   Open: Year-round

It used to be that after losing at the blackjack table, gamblers went to the bar to drown their sorrows. Not anymore. Now there's a healthier option: the casino spa. The Desert Inn's Italian-designed spa is a sure bet for winners and losers alike.

This spa typifies Las Vegas' own brand of opulence. Hand-painted frescoes depicting idyllic woodland scenes adorn the spa's entry hall, giving guests the illusion of being worlds away from the flash and glitter of the casino. The spa is the perfect place to renew oneself.

Half-day, one-day and four-day spa plans are available, or Desert Inn guests can use the facilities for $15 a day. All personal services, such as massage or facials, cost extra.

The spa offers daily exercise classes, personalized fitness and cardiovascular analysis, a multitude of beauty and relaxation treatments, a 2,100-square-foot gym, a weight training center and more. As an added touch, the spa provides warm-up clothes, robes, leotards, shorts, sandals and towels to all guests.

Activities & Services

Aerobics, stretch, aquacise, personalized fitness and cardiovascular analysis, weight training, massage, salt glow and loofah body scrubs, herbal wrap, paraffin treatment, dermatological complexion analysis, manicure, pedicure, full-service beauty and barber salon. Hot, warm and cool therapy pools, private whirlpools, Turkish steam room, sauna. Swimming, tennis, jogging track.

Lodging

The Desert Inn features newly renovated deluxe hotel rooms, with such amenities as shampoo and body lotion.

Cuisine

Although the Desert Inn doesn't serve low-calorie cuisine, low-calorie drinks are available in the spa. The inn has several restaurants.

WESTERN SPAS

MGM Desert Inn Hotel and Casino
3145 Las Vegas Boulevard South   702-733-4444
Las Vegas, NV 89109   800-634-6906

UTAH

THE CLIFF SPA

$$$
Snowbird, Utah   Open: Year-round

Serious skiers know Snowbird, Utah, as a first-rate ski resort. Snowbird is equally well-known to spa-goers for the renowned Cliff Spa, located on the top two floors of The Cliff Lodge.

First-time visitors are in for a surprise. One would imagine a Bavarian-style inn, quaint and charming. Instead, The Cliff Spa is housed in a contemporary high-rise that looks more like a slick office building than a lodge.

Almost every room, from the guest rooms to the day-care center to the private massage rooms, has a floor-to-ceiling view of the beautiful mountains surrounding The Cliff Lodge. The tinted glass allows anyone inside to look out but prevents outsiders from looking in. Therefore, guests can peacefully enjoy the scenery, even when they're in the buff—precisely what the architect intended. The spa, decorated in the palest tints of pink and dove gray, is elegant and fresh, providing a subtle backdrop for the dramatic mountainscapes.

Every day a fitness schedule is posted with descriptions of each class. The spa offers daily exercise classes and complete instruction on the use and benefits of Keiser K-300 pneumatic air pressure weights and Lifecycles. A variety of different wraps and massages are available including parafango—a heat-retaining mixture of volcanic ash and paraffin, molded to such areas of the body as the back and shoulders to relax muscles. A back and shoulder pressure-point massage completes this treatment.

■ AFFORDABLE SPAS

Even though it's housed in The Cliff Lodge, the spa itself is very self-contained. Massage rooms, a full-service beauty salon, steam room, hydromassage and cedar-paneled herbal wrap rooms, and sauna are located on the spa's first floor. A stairway, only accessible from inside the spa, leads to the second-floor aerobics room with large corner windows that offer a panoramic view. Also upstairs are a weight room, stretching room, swimming pool, whirlpool and the Spa Cafe.

The spa offers a variety of different spa packages and prices, which vary according to the season. Guests can sign up for spa services and activities on an a la carte basis, which can get expensive.

Snowbird's summer off-season equals the popular ski season in many ways. The summer temperature rarely rises above 75 degrees. Wildflowers grace the mountains. And guests receive considerably more attention because the spa isn't crowded.

The Cliff Spa attracts a lot of skiers between the ages of 25 and 35 during the winter. Most of the off-season spa-goers are women.

The Cliff Spa just barely met the "affordable" pricing standards of this book. However, it's one of the most luxurious and professionally managed spas in the country and is well worth the cost.

Activities & Services

Stretch and flex (flexercise), controlled-impact aerobics, stress management, fitness evaluation, cardio-conditioning, Keiser K-300 equipment, aquacise, massage, hydromassage, herbal wraps, parafango, facial, manicure, pedicure, full-service beauty salon, mountain biking, swimming, skiing, rock climbing, tennis, evening hikes with campfire cookouts, backpacking. Child-care available for children three and older.

Lodging

The rooms are spacious and tastefully decorated. As a special touch, the bathtub has a picture window on one side so guests can enjoy the view while bathing.

Cuisine

Guests whose goal is dieting will want to stick to the Spa Cafe, which even serves wine for those who don't want to completely deprive themselves. Calorie counts are given for each item. Sample dishes from the menu include black pepper and parsley pasta, cold poached salmon with Dijon vinaigrette, vegetable pate, five different kinds of smoothies. For guests not interested in dieting, the lodge has several other restaurants, including The Aerie, a formal dining room; The Atrium, good for lunch and snacks; and a Mexican cafe.

The Cliff Spa
Snowbird, UT 84092   800-453-3000

NATIONAL INSTITUTE OF FITNESS

$$

Ivins, Utah   Open: Year-round

Those who've tried a lot of diets, only to gain the weight back again, might find the weight loss program at the National Institute of Fitness a refreshing change. The institute's philosophy: Diets don't work.

So what works? According to the institute, eating more—not less—of a diet high in fiber and complex carbohydrates and low in salt, sugar and oil. And, of course, exercise.

Most guests are shocked by what they get to eat at the institute. They're allowed to indulge in otherwise-forbidden foods, such as pancakes and mashed potatoes.

While everyone enjoys the cuisine at the institute, this is *not* one of those places where guests are coddled and pampered. The attitude is fairly serious. "This is a no-nonsense approach to a positive attitude through simplified nutrition and exercise," says NIF General Manager Jay Cooper. "Our staff is an upbeat group of optimists." Everyone focuses 100 percent of the program. The only distraction is the magnificent scenery.

Located at the mouth of Snow Canyon — a geological wonderland of towering red sandstone cliffs and canyons — the institute is housed in a complex of white geodesic domes. Juxtaposed against cinnamon-colored canyon walls and bright blue sky, it looks like the desert scene in *Star Wars*, a world both ancient and futuristic.

Upon arrival, guests receive a comprehensive fitness evaluation, which includes recording weight and testing blood pressure, body composition, flexibility and strength. Guests are placed in an A, B or C exercise group, depending upon their physical condition (determined by a cardiovascular endurance test).

Walking is the backbone of the program. Add to that various voluntary classes, including everything from aerobics, body sculpturing and swimming to lectures on the mathematics of fat. A record of a guest's progress is monitored and reviewed daily by the staff group leader.

The institute is popular with professional women in their late thirties and forties. Most guests are from large metropolitan areas.

Activities & Services

Aerobics, body sculpting, body contouring, aquacise, stretching, swimming, walking, cycling, mini-trampoline, racquetball, tennis, weight training. Cardiovascular training area including motorized treadmills and computerized exercise bicycles. Lectures on fat control, nutrition and fitness. Goal-setting and self-image improvement through behavior modification techniques.

Lodging

Accommodations in the institute's geodesic domes are simple, comfortable and immaculately clean.

Cuisine

A 900-calorie diet is served. However, guests aren't allowed to go hungry. If guests experience pangs, they're sometimes led to the kitchen for a snack. Men and high-endurance exercisers are allotted enough calories to maintain a high energy level. Popular dishes include turkey with dressing and mashed potatoes, stir-fry vegetables and whole grain pancakes.

National Institute of Fitness
202 N. Snow Canyon Road
P.O. Box H
Ivins, UT 84738   801-628-3317

WASHINGTON

ROSARIO ISLAND RESORT AND SPA
$$
Eastsound, Washington   **Open: Year-round**

Located on pine-studded Orcas Island off the coast of Washington, Rosario Island Resort and Spa sits perched on a bluff, overlooking a cove. The landscape is rugged and romantic with meadows shrouded in mist, craggy cliffs rising out of the Pacific Ocean and acres of emerald forest.

Part of the San Juan Islands in Puget Sound, Orcas, like many of the nearby islands, has remained relatively untouched by tourism. The only way to get there is by plane, sea plane or ferry—and getting there is half the fun.

Built at the turn of the century by Seattle shipbuilder Robert Moran, Rosario occupies a large white mansion that still maintains its original charm. The house, which has been

AFFORDABLE SPAS

renovated over the years, still has some of the Mission oak furniture, popular when Moran built Rosario.

Also unchanged is a spectacular organ room with stained glass windows and cathedral ceilings where Moran entertained family and friends. It's now used for historic lectures and organ concerts.

Rosario's spa program focuses more on stress reduction than weight loss. Various exercise classes are offered daily. Also featured is a wide range of massage and body wrap treatments, some inspired by the sea, such as the body glow rub with fragrant oils, salt and algae for exfoliating.

During the summer, Rosario attracts a diverse clientele — couples, families, senior citizens. It's a great place to take children, even infants. Most summer guests don't visit Rosario for the spa program, but rather to enjoy swimming, relaxing, hiking and touring the island.

During fall and winter, Rosario offers special packages that attract more spa-goers. The off-season environment is more intimate, subdued and relaxed.

Activities & Services

Stretch and tone (flexercise), low-impact aerobics, aquacise, dance exercise, massage (Trager, shiatsu, reflexology, multiple, Swedish and rollerbed), yoga, guided visualization, body awakening (helps correct posture), aromatherapy facials, body wraps, lymphatic cleansing, aromatic steam, salt glow rub, tanning bed, full-service beauty salon, swimming, hiking, boating.

Lodging

Unfortunately, guests can't stay in the mansion. Accommodations are in lodges hidden among the pine trees on a hill overlooking the harbor. The rooms are large and most have patios.

Cuisine

Chef William Jung's spa menu includes a wide range of dishes, such as grilled salmon with peppercorn, basil and red pepper sauce; chicken wrapped in romaine; green salad with fresh fruit juice and cayenne pepper dressing; grilled rabbit marinated in curry and yogurt. Those who aren't dieting can feast at breakfast, lunch and dinner on the resort's regular cuisine, which is as beautiful and abundant as the scenery.

Rosario Island Resort and Spa 206-376-2222
Eastsound, WA 98245 800-562-8820 (WA)

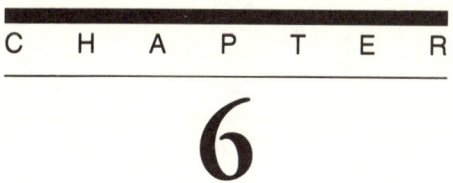

CHAPTER 6

Weekend Spa Getaways

6

TGIF

Busy schedule? No time for a vacation? Then it may be time to pack your weekend bag, cancel the Sunday *Times* and head for the nearest spa.

Many spas feature special weekend packages that give people a respite from their daily routines. In general, weekend programs offer guests a lot of flexibility in choosing activities and services. After all, some weekend spa-goers want to relax and be pampered, while others want a vigorous workout.

Weekend packages also can provide a good introduction to spas. The previously uninitiated have an opportunity to experience spas without the expense and time commitment involved in a week-long stay.

Below is a listing of some spas offering weekend packages. (In-depth descriptions of each spa can be found in Chapters Two through Five, categorized by geographical region.) Because weekend programs and rates change frequently, contact the spas for more information on their specific weekend programs.

■ AFFORDABLE SPAS

THE WEEKEND DIRECTORY

THE ASPEN CLUB

1450 Crystal Lake Road
Aspen, CO 81611

$$$/Summer and Fall
Open: Year-round

303-925-6760
800-443-2582 (CO)
800-882-2582 (out of state)

THE SPA AT BALLY'S

Bally's Park Place Casino
   Hotel
Park Place and Boardwalk
Atlantic City, NJ 08401

$$ and $$$
Open: Year-round

609-340-4600
800-772-7777

BIRDWING SPA

Rural Route 2
Box 99
Litchfield, MN 55355

$$
Open: Year-round

612-693-6064

**BREAK AWAY TOTAL HEALTH
   AND FITNESS RESORT**

P.O. Box 1868
Sandpoint, ID 83864

$$$
Open: Spring, Fall, Winter

208-263-3194
800-635-2534 (out of state)

WEEKEND SPA GETAWAYS

DEERFIELD MANOR

R.D. 1
Route 402
East Stroudsburg, PA 18301

$
Open: May to November

717-223-0160

**THE FONTAINEBLEU HILTON
   RESORT AND SPA**

4441 Collins Avenue
Miami Beach, FL 33140

$$$/Summer
Open: Year-round

305-538-2000
800-HILTONS

**FOUR SEASONS HOTEL
   AND RESORT**

4150 North MacArthur Blvd.
Irving, TX 75038

$$$
Open: Year-round

214-717-0700

THE GLASS DOOR SPA

Sugar Loaf Hill
Natrona Heights, PA 15065

$$$
Open: Year-round

412-826-1422

**GUADALUPE RIVER RANCH
   AND HEALTH
   ENHANCEMENT CENTER**

P.O. Box 929
Boerne, TX 78006

$$$/Weekends
Open: Year-round

512-698-1592

AFFORDABLE SPAS

THE HEARTLAND $$$/Weekends
Open: Year-round

Gilman, Illinois

Direct all correspondence and phone inquiries to The Heartland business office:

18 East Chestnut Street 312-266-2050
Suite 200
Chicago, IL 60611

THE HOMESTEAD $$$
Open: Year-round

Hot Springs, VA 24445 703-839-5500
800-542-5734 (VA)
800-336-5771 (out of state)

KRIPALU CENTER $ and $$
Open: Year-round

Box 793 413-637-3280
Lenox, MA 01240

MAYFAIR: THE SPA BY THE SEA $$ and $$$
Open: Year-round

105 S. Little Rock Avenue 609-487-8083
Ventnor, NJ 08406

WEEKEND SPA GETAWAYS

NEW AGE HEALTH FARM

Route 55
Neversink, NY 12765

$, $$ and $$$
Open: Year-round

914-985-7601
800-682-4348 (NY)

NORWICH INN AND SPA

Route 32
Norwich, CT 06360

$$$
Open: Year-round

203-886-2401
800-892-5692

**OLYMPIA VILLAGE
CONFERENCE CENTER
RESORT SPA**

1350 Royal Mile Road
Oconomowoc, WI 53066

$$ and $$$
Open: Year-round

414-567-0311
800-558-9573

**OMEGA INSTITUTE FOR
HOLISTIC STUDIES**

R.D. 2
Box 377
Rhinebeck, NY 12572

$
Open: Summer

914-266-4301 (May 15 to
   September 15)
914-338-6030 (September 16
   to May 14)

LE PARKER MERIDIEN

118 West 57th Street
New York, NY 10019

$$$/Weekends
Open: Year-round

212-245-5000
800-543-4300

177

AFFORDABLE SPAS

SAFETY HARBOR SPA AND FITNESS CENTER

$$$/Summer
Open: Year-round

105 N. Bayshore Drive
Safety Harbor, FL 34695

813-726-1161
800-237-0155

TENNANAH LAKESHORE LODGE SPA AND RETREAT

$ and $$
Open: Year-round

R.D. 2
Box 71
Roscoe, NY 12776

607-498-4900
800-922-LAKE

CHAPTER 7

The Spa Suitcase

7

Tips on What to Pack

Forget black leotards and gray sweat pants. Those are the cheerless predecessors of today's colorful athletic wear. And what better place to wear the exciting new generation of workout clothes than at a spa.

Not all spas advocate wearing the latest athletic fashions. A two-tone pink and aqua spandex leotard with a silver sash and matching headband would probably be out of place at some spas, particularly holistic retreats where the spiritual is of more concern than the style.

However, many spas encourage guests to wear comfortable, functional clothes that look fashionable, too.

Whether you're headed for a super spa such as Palm-Aire in Florida or a more rustic retreat such as Akia in Oklahoma, you won't have to pack a lot of clothes, just the basics listed below.

If you forget something or need a smaller size when the pounds start to fall away, many spas sell athletic wear.

Even though most spas have laundry facilities, take some Woolite along so you can wash personal items in your hotel bathroom.

AFFORDABLE SPAS

The basics, for starters:
- Leotards
- Tights
- Gym shorts
- Warm-ups
- T-shirts
- Sweat suit
- Running or aerobic shoes (well broken-in)
- Bathing suit
- Cover-up or caftan
- Casual clothes for evening (see below)
- Hat or visor
- Tote/gym bag
- Socks, socks, and more socks (two pair per day)
- Sweat band and/or covered ponytail holders

Depending upon the spa's location and the weather, consider the following:
- Light or heavy jacket
- Raincoat
- Umbrella
- Shoes for muddy walks

Don't forget the often-neglected miscellaneous items:
- Sunscreen for face and body
- Camera and film
- Writing paper and stamps
- Aspirin (Most spas serve decaffeinated coffee. If you're used to the real thing, caffeine withdrawal can result in headaches.)
- Beach towel, if not provided by spa

What to wear after hours:
The evening dress code at all standard spas is casual—warm-ups or shorts and t-shirt. However, some spas are considerably more informal than others. At Russell House in Key West, Florida, dinner attire includes wet bathing

THE SPA SUITCASE

suits. On the other hand, at Safety Harbor in Tampa, women don rhinestone-studded warm-ups accented with gold lame flowers while the men wear sports shirts and slacks.

The evening dress code at resort spas is more formal. Male guests tend toward the resortwear look — casual pants and a stylish shirt and sport jacket — while women dress in belted t-shirt dresses or linen pants and blouses.

Lycra and Other Fashion Wonders

Surveying the fashions in the workout rooms brings to mind comedian Billy Crystal's famous maxim: "It's more important to look mah-velous than to feel mah-velous." Spa-goers go all-out in the leotard-and-tights department.

In exercise classes at spas across the nation, men and women sport workout clothes in every shape, style and color combination imaginable. Some styles are beautiful, others outrageous, and some look like creations from Frederick's of Hollywood. There's a look to satisfy everyone's taste.

For women, leotard styles vary from plunging backs and fronts to turtle necks, and every neck style in between. Some are cut out on the side of the waist. Stretchy sashes accentuate the waist even when there isn't much of one. Many leotards are cut high on the thigh to make the legs look longer.

The colors are flattering and fun — peach, canary, aqua, lavender, fuschia, dove gray, tobacco brown, gold, silver, copper, you name it.

There are even fashionable solutions for what to do with your hair while you're working up a sweat. Stretchy headbands are available in a multitude of colors and styles. They don't pull or flatten your hair.

Leotards, tights, headbands, aerobics shoes and matching tote bags can all be purchased in any major

183

AFFORDABLE SPAS

department or athletic store. The prices of leotards and tights vary, depending on the fabric.

The ideal material for aerobic and bicycling wear is lycra and/or spandex. If you've never worn those space-age fabrics, you're in for a surprise. They smooth and mold your body contour, just like an old-fashioned girdle. But with these fabrics, you have total freedom of movement and can breathe. The fabrics make your body look noticeably slimmer (up to seven pounds lighter, according to many assessments). Nothing shakes or wiggles. These fabrics cost more, but they're well worth the price.

If you already have a couple of spandex or lycra leotards and tights, consider buying a new one or two, particularly if you're staying for a week or longer. Chances are you'll be in a leotard at least twice a day. It's nice to have some choices in both style, color and, above all, freshness.

Beauty, Skincare and Haircare for the Spa-goer

Some women find the notion of wearing makeup while exercising ludicrous. However, many spas actually encourage the use of light makeup, particularly for those who aren't used to seeing themselves without it.

Staring into all those floor-to-ceiling mirrors in the aerobics/exercise room day after day makes most women very conscious of how they look. A little makeup can provide a psychological boost, inspiring some people to try harder. The same principle applies with attractive clothing.

On the other hand, some women don't even want to think about makeup or clothes. Both ways are acceptable at most spas.

If you belong to the makeup-in-the-exercise-room school of thought, consider using the following:

    Waterproof mascara
    Eye makeup remover
    Lipstick with sunscreen
    Oil-free foundation with sunscreen

Eye makeup remover is important because waterproof mascara is difficult to remove with just soap and water or moisturizer. An oil-free foundation is less likely to clog pores and run while you perspire.

Regardless of the sage advice of the salesperson behind the cosmetic counter, eye shadow and exercise don't mix. As you work up a sweat, eye shadow tends to cake up. Neither do lip gloss and exercise mix well. Blush isn't really necessary. After all, the exercise and good clean living give you a natural blush.

Most spa-goers shower at least twice a day. You may need to double the amount of shampoo, conditioner and moisturizer you normally use. You really go through those products at a spa. Consider using a gentle shampoo designed for frequent use and a light conditioner that won't leave heavy deposits on the hair.

Glossary

Glossary

Improve Your Spa Vocabulary

Salt glow, herbal wrap and aromatherapy might sound like cooking terms, but they're among the many personal services offered in most spas. The spa world has a vocabulary all its own. For example, you don't have to be in a hotel in Zurich to take a Swiss shower. Nor do you show up at a parcourse with golf clubs. This glossary provides definitions for some services and programs typically offered at spas and fitness resorts.

Acupressure: To stimulate the flow of energy throughout the body, finger pressure is applied to specific points of the body, thought to correspond to vital organs (the same points used in acupuncture). Acupressure massage is similar in many ways to shiatsu.

Acupuncture: This ancient Chinese system involves the insertion of needles at different points of the body, thought to be linked to various vital organs. It isn't as painful as it sounds. In fact, acupuncture is most commonly used to treat chronic pain.

Affirmation: Similar to visualization, this technique is used to overcome physical ailments (e.g., backaches) and emotional problems (e.g., family or professional problems) by repeating a positive statement. For example, a person who is afraid of flying would repeat "I like to fly" and envision a pleasant flying experience.

Alexander Technique: Most people stand and move in imbalanced ways that result in a multitude of physical problems, such as backaches. This technique teaches you how to move with greater ease and coordination by focusing on correct posture, the right way to lift objects, the proper position of feet when standing, the angle of one's shoulders and so forth.

Aquacise: Aquacise is aerobics done in a swimming pool, although it sometimes refers to other types of pool exercises. At many spas, this is the most popular exercise class. It's fun, easy and sweat-free. The fact that most of us look more graceful in the water than on an exercise mat probably contributes to aquacise's popularity.

Aromatherapy: An ancient healing art dating back to 4500 B.C., aromatherapy usually refers to a massage with essential oils from plants, leaves, bark, roots, seeds, resins and flowers gently rubbed into the skin. It refreshes and relaxes the skin and soothes the mind.

Behavior Modification: This is one of the most effective forms of therapy for treating eating disorders and helping

SPA GLOSSARY

smokers to kick cigarettes by correcting ingrained habits. Most spas incorporate behavior modification into their weight loss program. Instead of prescribing to a special diet, the behavior modification approach teaches people how to change lifelong eating habits so they can still enjoy all types of food, but within reason.

Biofeedback: Various machines teach you how to voluntarily control muscle tension, stomach acidity, heart rate and other autonomic responses. Biofeedback is commonly used to treat stress-related conditions such as asthma, insomnia, high blood pressure, migraines. It also can teach you how to relax.

Body Composition: This test (usually part of an overall fitness analysis) determines the percentage of body fat by using a skin-fold caliper (a measuring instrument) that gently pinches the skin below the underarm.

Body Contour: Body contour exercises work on specific parts of the body—such as the abdomen, buttocks, hips and thighs—for toning, increased flexibility and mobility.

Body Tuning: Stretching and muscle firming exercises.

Body Work: This refers to all forms of therapeutic touch, such as massage.

Brush and Tone: The body is brushed in invigorating, circular motions to remove dead skin and increase circulation. It feels like the world's greatest back scratch, all over your body. Moisturizing lotion is applied afterward. Brush and tone is sometimes called dry brush massage.

AFFORDABLE SPAS

Cardiovascular Testing and Training: The degree of testing and training varies widely from spa to spa. The maximum stress test with electrocardiogram evaluation is performed on a treadmill to detect the possible presence of heart disease, determine the heart's capacity to pump and help provide guidelines for an exercise program. Sometimes body composition and vital capacity also are tested. Training and testing equipment includes Lifecycles, rowing ergometers, Versa Climbers, Stair Masters, stationary bikes, Nordic trainer and Quinton treadmills.

Circuit Training: This personally assisted weight training program uses a variety of equipment such as Nautilus, Universal or Keiser.

Color Analysis: Think you look good in blue? A color analysis may prove otherwise. Each season of the year represents a group of colors that are flattering to certain skin tones. To determine whether you're a spring, summer, fall or winter color type, swatches of fabric from each season are held next to your face. The analysis, based on the colors that are most becoming to you, then gives you guidelines for choosing wardrobe and makeup colors.

Creative Movement: This includes dance, aerobic and stretch exercises designed to improve your coordination and mobility.

Creative Visualization: This relaxation technique is similar to hypnosis except you remain conscious. It's usually done with a group of people lying in a quiet, dark room. In a soft, even-toned voice, an instructor asks the group to imagine themselves in a serene, relaxing environment, such as a beautiful sandy beach or peaceful meadow. By describing things like the color of the sky or the smell of wildflowers, the instructor creates a soothing fantasy environment. About half the group falls asleep; the other half goes into a state of deep relaxation. Visualization is also used to treat phobias by having people imagine successfully doing whatever it is they fear.

Deep Muscle Massage (sometimes called deep tissue massage): This massage is a deep, sometimes painful kneading of the muscles. The best-known types of deep muscle massage include Rolfing, Reichian and Benjamin. It's not for everyone; some people find deep muscle massage very uncomfortable and not the least bit relaxing. Its proponents, however, claim that the massage has ample benefits (e.g. improved posture and relief of chronic tension).

Deep Tissue Massage: See Deep Muscle Massage.

Dry Brush Massage: See Brush and Tone.

Esalen Massage: Developed and refined over the last 20 years by Esalen Institute in California, this massage combines Swedish and sensory relaxation massage techniques. This soothing and comforting massage utilizes long, full-handed strokes.

Facial: A standard facial usually includes massaging the face, cleansing, toning, steaming, exfoliating and moisturizing. Other types of facials, masks and skin treatments are available at most spas. They include a European facial (similar to a standard facial except the products are European); a peeling mask designed to lift dead skin and encourage new skin growth; a paraffin mask, which helps increase circulation and rehydrate the skin; and a deep cleansing facial that purifies and revitalizes the skin.

Fango Bath: Fango means mud in Italian, but this isn't the type that's suitable for mud pies. Believe it or not, this is fancy mud. Fango creates an all-encompassing, gooey warmth and works like a poultice, softening the skin. Natural ingredients, such as peat moss and sea kelp, often are mixed into the mud to help contain the warmth and increase mineral content. Sometimes fango is applied to tense parts of the body, such as the shoulders. Other fango baths are just that — a dip in a tub filled with mud (an experience not to be missed). Some types of mud harden on the skin. Others remain moist. Occasionally mud is mixed with paraffin to produce "parafango," which relaxes the body, alleviates sore muscles and softens the skin.

Fitness Evaluation: Depending on the spa, this usually involves evaluating cardiovascular fitness, flexibility, muscular fitness and body composition. Results enable the spa to design an individualized program, based on personal goals, abilities and lifestyle.

Flexercise (sometimes called stretch and tone or stretch and flex): These gentle stretching exercises increase flexibility. A popular early morning activity, flexercise helps you wake up and prepare yourself for more rigorous exercise later on.

Flotation/Isolation Tank: This enclosed tank, containing warm water and Epsom salts, allows you to float comfortably in a totally dark, silent environment. This can be a serene, deeply relaxing experience for some, but claustrophobic for others. It creates a sensation that has been likened to returning to the womb.

Guided Visualization: See Creative Visualization.

SPA GLOSSARY

Hand and Foot Treatment: This often includes a standard manicure and pedicure, followed by a seaweed or paraffin mask to soften and smooth the skin.

Herbal Wrap: Your body is wrapped in warm linen or cotton sheets that have been steeped like tea bags in a variety of aromatic herbs. You're then covered with blankets or towels, which prevent the moist heat from escaping. Herbal wraps help relax the muscles, soothe soreness and soften skin. However, some people find the heat oppressive and the cocoon effect of the wet sheets and blankets smothering. To avoid feeling claustrophobic, you can leave your arms outside of the wrap.

Holistic Health: Some spas offer programs based on holistic health principles. The definition of "health" is the absence of illness. "Holistic health" is based on physical, mental and social well-being — which holistic health advocates believe are interconnected. When one is out of sync, the others are affected. For instance, even regular exercise and nutritionally balanced meals don't make up for a mentally troubled state. Holistic-oriented spas often teach ancient Eastern systems such as T'ai Chi and yoga, as well as Western systems such as biofeedback, to induce relaxation.

Hydrotherapy Pools: This generally refers to an underwater massage in a multijet tub, an exhilarating experience. It also can mean a whirlpool bath, hot Roman pool, hot tub, Jacuzzi, cold plunge and mineral bath.

Inhalation Room: Eucalyptus or herbs are used to open the sinuses and make breathing easier.

Loofah: Once dried, this natural plant looks like a mutant piece of shredded wheat, but it doesn't feel scratchy. It's used to slough off dead skin, and is particularly effective after a sauna.

Low-impact Aerobics: Most spas offer low-impact aerobics—exercise movements in which one foot always remains on the ground, lessening the impact and avoiding physical injury. Low-impact is easier and safer to do than high-impact aerobics, which involves a lot of jumping, skipping, hopping and jogging. Some spas offer high-impact aerobics, but usually only to advanced students.

Lymph Massage: Sometimes called lymphatic drainage massage, it requires serious knowledge of the location of the lymph nodes. Be sure the masseuse or masseur knows what she/he's doing. Sometimes done on the face and neck, other times the entire body, lymph massage helps stimulate lymphatic circulation, which boosts the body's ability to eliminate wastes and absorb nutrients. It can also reduce swollen or puffy tissue and tone underlying tissue.

Makeup Consultation: This usually involves learning to apply makeup appropriate for your skin type, look and age. If this isn't a spa's area of expertise, you may be disappointed with the results. However, if the spa has a full-service beauty salon, the results probably will be pleasing.

Meditation: Often used as part of a stress reduction program, meditation is usually done in a peaceful setting outdoors or in a quiet room, away from distracting sounds and sights. Meditators assume a comfortable sitting position. An instructor tells meditators to concentrate on breathing in a slow, rhythmic motion, imagining the release

SPA GLOSSARY

of tension as they exhale. Often a simple word (or mantra) is repeated with each breath. The general purpose is to relax the body and quiet the ongoing chatter of the conscious mind. Practice is required to meditate effectively, but the physical benefits are well worth it. Meditation decreases the heart rate, oxygen consumption, blood pressure, blood lactate levels, muscle tension and metabolic rate. It increases alpha brain waves, alertness, awareness, creativity and psychological well-being.

Musculoskeletal Health Assessment: This often involves examining range of motion, muscle strength, posture, gaits, flexibility and skeletal alignment in order to focus on problem areas that might require special exercises.

Orthion Machine: Your entire body, even your head, is strapped to this mechanical massage table (Frankenstein revisited). The table then gently pulls, stretches, lifts and massages strategic points to help loosen and relax muscles. The duration and degree of movement is controlled by an attendant who operates a rather elaborate control panel on the side of the table—further contributing to the Frankenstein image.

Panthermal: You lie in this fat metal tube that resembles an iron lung. Hot dry air circulates around your body (your head is outside the tube) and you work up quite a sweat. Gentle jets of warm soapy water then hit you from all directions. Panthermal is designed to break down cellulite. It's not recommended for people who get claustrophobic.

Parcourse: This reminds some people of a civilian version of an obstacle course at military boot camp. It consists on an outdoor jogging track with 12 to 18 different exercise obstacles that are designed to increase balance, agility, flexibility and body awareness.

Polarity Massage: This relatively new form of massage balances the body's energy systems via gentle manipulations and relaxation techniques.

Race Walking: This brisk, exaggerated, aerobic form of walking looks like exercise on a cartoon, but helps develop stomach, thigh and buttock muscle tone.

Radu: Radu is rigorous, low-impact aerobics for advanced students that utilizes hand weights, sticks and low benches.

Release and Balance: Stretching exercise that releases energy and improves posture.

Reflexology: Reflexology refers to a foot, hand or ear massage. However, most spas only concentrate on feet. It's based upon the theory that each body organ is represented by a corresponding reflex point on your foot. For instance, the point for the thyroid is the bottom part of the big toes. Massaging the proper points of the feet and ankles releases energy throughout the body, not to mention the effect it has on aching feet.

Salt Glow: A vigorous, abrasive scrub—consisting of crunchy salt usually mixed with essential oils and water—cleanses pores and removes dead skin. It's usually followed by a gentle shower and body moisturizer.

Scalp and Hair Treatment: The products used vary from spa to spa. Some use natural ingredients, such as a sea kelp mixture; others use chemically based products. However, the process and result are generally the same: a thorough

SPA GLOSSARY

cleansing, conditioning and scalp massage that leave hair shiny and full of body.

Scotch Water Massage: Sixteen needle-spray shower heads and two high-pressure hoses (operated by an attendant), ranging in temperature from 45 to 105 degrees, hit you simultaneously. This massage aids circulation and helps relieve the pain of arthritis and rheumatism. It's stimulating; however, some people feel silly standing naked while an attendant blasts them with two big hoses.

Shiatsu Massage: Thumb or finger pressure is applied to the same trigger points of the body used in acupressure. It increases the body's flow of energy, helps eliminate blockages and feels extraordinarily good.

Skin Glow Rub: Skin is softened with a sauna, then mineral water and sometimes salt are massaged into the skin, leaving it soft and glowing.

Sports Stretch: Stretching exercises to limber up and better prepare the body for rigorous athletics. (Similar to a football warm-up.)

Stress Management: Most spas offer a variety of tension-relieving techniques that fall under the category of stress management (yoga, meditation, guided relaxation and visualization, stretching and breathing exercises, positive thinking, and nutritional counseling).

Stretch and Flex: See Flexercise.

Stretch and Tone: See Flexercise.

AFFORDABLE SPAS

Swedish Massage: Of all the massage techniques, this is the most popular. It employs kneading, pounding and rubbing movements to induce relaxation.

Swimnastics: Water exercises to slim and tone the body.

Swiss Shower: Fourteen shower sprays, ranging in temperature from 60 to 150 degrees, hit you from all directions simultaneously. It's an exhilarating experience that stimulates the nerve endings and makes you hop up and down.

T'ai Chi: This ancient Chinese system looks like a slow-motion dance of graceful movements and deep, relaxed breathing. It's sort of a mobile meditation, used for health, relaxation, self defense and to induce energy. It's widely practiced in the Orient by people of all ages.

Thalassotherapy: A seaweed body wrap helps restore elasticity and minerals and eliminate toxins. As with most wraps, it usually involves seaweed paste rubbed on the body, which is then covered with sheets and sometimes blankets for 10 to 20 minutes.

Touch and Tone: Exercises to firm the body.

Trager Body Work: Developed by Hawaiian physician Dr. Milton Trager, this massage form uses gentle, sometimes deep, rhythmic, rocking movements to release tension.

Visualization: See Creative Visualization.

Yoga: An ancient Hindu system of stretching, breathing and meditative exercises, yoga is frequently part of stress-reduction programs. It helps improve muscle tone, flexibility and mobility; reduces stress and anxiety; and induces a sense of well-being.

Index

Akia, 109
The Aspen Club, 149, 174
Avenue Plaza Hotel/EuroVita Spa, 78

The Spa at Bally's, 23, 174
Bermuda Inn Fitness and Reducing Resort, 127
Birdwing Spa, 106, 174
Bluegrass Spa, 76
Break Away Total Health and Fitness Resort, 159, 174

Carmel Country Spa, 129
The Cliff Spa, 163
Coolfont Resort, 90

Deerfield Manor, 43, 175

Evernew Summer Spa Camp for Women, 19

The Fontainebleu Hilton Resort and Spa, 59, 175
Four Seasons Hotel and Resort, 80, 175

AFFORDABLE SPAS

The Spa at French Lick Springs Golf
   and Tennis Resort, 102

The Glass Door Spa, 45, 175
Golden Eagle Health Spa, 49
Grand Lake Spa Hotel, 11
The Greenbrier, 92
Guadalupe River Ranch
   and Health Enhancement Center, 82, 175

Harbor Island Spa (FL), 61
Harbor Island Spa (NJ), 25
Hartland Health Center, 86
The Heartland, 99, 176
The Himalayan Institute, 47
The Homestead, 88, 176

Interlaken Resort and Country Spa, 111

Kalani Honua Intercultural Retreat
   and Conference Center, 157
Kripalu Center, 21, 176

Lake Austin Resort Spa, 84
Lakeside Health Resort, 130
Lido Spa Hotel, 63
Living Springs Retreat, 30
Loews Ventana Canyon Resort, 119

Mayfair: The Spa by the Sea, 26, 176
Meadowlark Health and Growth Center, 132
MGM Desert Inn Hotel and Casino, 161
Mohonk Mountain House, 31
Monaco Villa Resort Hotel and Spa, 134
Mountain Meadows Center, 152

INDEX

Murrieta Hot Springs Resort, Spa and Conference Center, 136

National Institute of Fitness, 165
New Age Health Farm, 34, 177
New Life Spa, 51
Northern Pines Health Resort, 17
Norwich Inn and Spa, 13, 177

The Oaks at Ojai, 138
Olympia Village Conference Center Resort Spa, 113, 177
Omega Institute for Holistic Studies, 36, 177

The Spa at Palm-Aire, 67
The Palms at Palm Springs, 140
Palm Springs Spa Hotel and Mineral Springs, 142
Le Parker Meridien, 38, 177
Pawling Health Manor, 40

Regency Health Resort and Spa, 69
Rocky Mountain Wellness Spa, 153
Rosario Island Resort and Spa, 167
Russell House, 70

Safety Harbor Spa and Fitness Center, 72, 178
Sans Souci Health Resort, 107
Scottsdale Hilton Resort and Spa, 121
The Shoreham Hotel, 28
Sonesta Sanibel Harbour Resort, 74
The Spa at Stowe, 53

Tennanah Lakeshore Lodge Spa and Retreat, 42, 178
Tucson National Resort and Spa, 123

AFFORDABLE SPAS

Vail Hotel and Athletic Club, 156

Weight Watchers at The Bartley House, 104
Weight Watchers at The Camelview
 Radisson Resort, 125
Weight Watchers at The Newport Pier
 Holiday Inn, 65
Weight Watchers at The Surfside Inn, 144
Weight Watchers at The Hartford
 Treadway Hotel, 15
Wilbur Hot Springs Health Sanctuary, 146
The Wooden Door, 114
The Woods Fitness Institute, 94

Zane Haven, 147

Spas by State

Arizona
    Loews Ventana Canyon Resort, Tucson
    Scottsdale Hilton Resort and Spa, Scottsdale
    Tucson National Resort and Spa, Tucson
    Weight Watchers at The Camelview Radisson Resort, Scottsdale

California
    Bermuda Inn Fitness and Reducing Resort, Lancaster
    Carmel Country Spa, Carmel Valley
    Lakeside Health Resort, Lake Elsinore
    Meadowlark Health and Growth Center, Hemet
    Monaco Villa Resort Hotel and Spa, Palm Springs
    Murrieta Hot Springs Resort, Spa and Conference Center, Murrieta
    The Oaks at Ojai, Ojai
    The Palms at Palm Springs, Palm Springs
    Palm Springs Spa Hotel and Mineral Springs,

AFFORDABLE SPAS

    Palm Springs
Weight Watchers at The Surfside Inn,
    Santa Barbara
Wilbur Hot Springs Health Sanctuary,
    Williams
Zane Haven, Palm Springs

Colorado

The Aspen Club, Aspen
Mountain Meadows Center, Jamestown
Rocky Mountain Wellness Spa,
    Steamboat Springs
Vail Hotel and Athletic Club, Vail

Connecticut

Grand Lake Spa Hotel, Lebanon
Norwich Inn and Spa, Norwich
Weight Watchers at The Hartford
    Treadway Hotel, Cromwell

Florida

The Fontainebleu Hilton Resort and Spa,
    Miami Beach
Harbor Island Spa, North Bay Village
Lido Spa Hotel, Miami Beach
Palm-Aire Resort and Spa, Pompano Beach
Regency Health Resort and Spa, Hallandale
Russell House, Key West
Safety Harbor Spa and Fitness Center,
    Safety Harbor
Sonesta Sanibel Harbour Resort, Fort Myers
Weight Watchers at The Newport Pier
    Holiday Inn, Miami Beach

Hawaii

Kalani Honua Intercultural Retreat

and Conference Center, Kalapana Beach

Illinois
The Heartland, Gilman

Indiana
The Spa at French Lick Springs Golf and Tennis Resort, French Lick

Idaho
Break Away Total Health and Fitness Resort, Sandpoint

Kentucky
Bluegrass Spa, Stamping Ground

Louisiana
Avenue Plaza Hotel/EuroVita Spa, New Orleans

Maine
Northern Pines Health Resort, Raymond

Massachusetts
Evernew Summer Spa Camp for Women, Milton Village
Kripalu Center, Lenox

Michigan
Weight Watchers at The Bartley House, Harbor Springs

Minnesota
Birdwing Spa, Litchfield

Nevada
MGM Desert Inn Hotel and Casino,

AFFORDABLE SPAS

    Las Vegas

New Jersey
    The Spa at Bally's, Atlantic City
    Harbor Island Spa, West End
    Mayfair: The Spa by the Sea, Ventnor
    The Shoreham Hotel, Spring Lake

New York
    Living Springs Retreat, Putnam Valley
    Mohonk Mountain House, New Paltz
    New Age Health Farm, Neversink
    Omega Institute for Holistic Studies, Rhinebeck
    Le Parker Meridien, New York
    Pawling Health Manor, Hyde Park
    Tennanah Lakeshore Lodge Spa and Retreat, Roscoe

Ohio
    Sans Souci Health Resort, Bellbrook

Oklahoma
    Akia, Sulphur

Pennsylvania
    Deerfield Manor, East Stroudsburg
    The Glass Door Spa, Natrona Heights
    The Himalayan Institute, Honesdale

Texas
    Four Seasons Hotel and Resort, Irving
    Guadalupe River Ranch and Health Enhancement Center, Boerne
    Lake Austin Resort Spa, Austin

SPAS BY STATE

Utah
 The Cliff Spa, Snowbird
 National Institute of Fitness, Ivins

Vermont
 Golden Eagle Health Spa, Stowe
 New Life Spa, Stratton Mountain
 The Spa at Stowe, Stowe

Virginia
 Hartland Health Center, Rapidan
 The Homestead, Hot Springs

Washington
 Rosario Resort and Spa, Eastsound

West Virginia
 Coolfont Resort, Berkeley Springs
 The Greenbrier, White Sulphur Springs
 The Woods Fitness Institute, Hedgesville

Wisconsin
 Interlaken Resort and Country Spa,
  West Lake Geneva
 Olympia Village Conference Center
  Resort Spa, Oconomowoc
 The Wooden Door, Lake Geneva

BEST SPA/RESORT VACATIONS

We appreciate any information you can supply about a spa/resort vacation you've recently taken. Detailed information about the spa programs, services, classes, staff, lodging, accommodations, cuisine and setting would be of interest to us. Describe daily activities, health-related programs and nearby points of interest. Finally, how did you hear about the spa, and how long have you been going there?

We'll be happy to send you a complimentary copy of the next edition of the book if we use your descriptions.

SEND TO: Ventana Press
P.O. Box 2468
Chapel Hill, NC 27515
919/490-0062

Spa/Resort: _____

Address: _____

_____ Zip: _____

Telephone: _____

Description: _____

_____

_____

_____

_____

Your name: _____ Telephone: _____

Address: _____

_____ Zip: _____

BEST SPA/RESORT VACATIONS

We appreciate any information you can supply about a spa/resort vacation you've recently taken. Detailed information about the spa programs, services, classes, staff, lodging, accommodations, cuisine and setting would be of interest to us. Describe daily activities, health-related programs and nearby points of interest. Finally, how did you hear about the spa, and how long have you been going there?

We'll be happy to send you a complimentary copy of the next edition of the book if we use your descriptions.

SEND TO: Ventana Press
P.O. Box 2468
Chapel Hill, NC 27515
919/490-0062

Spa/Resort: _____

Address: _____

_____ Zip: _____

Telephone: _____

Description: _____

_____

_____

_____

_____

_____

Your name: _____ Telephone: _____

Address: _____

_____ Zip: _____

BEST SPA/RESORT VACATIONS

We appreciate any information you can supply about a spa/resort vacation you've recently taken. Detailed information about the spa programs, services, classes, staff, lodging, accommodations, cuisine and setting would be of interest to us. Describe daily activities, health-related programs and nearby points of interest. Finally, how did you hear about the spa, and how long have you been going there?

We'll be happy to send you a complimentary copy of the next edition of the book if we use your descriptions.

    SEND TO: Ventana Press
                          P.O. Box 2468
                          Chapel Hill, NC 27515
                          919/490-0062

Spa/Resort: _____

Address: _____

_____ Zip: _____

Telephone: _____

Description: _____

_____

_____

_____

_____

_____

Your name: _____ Telephone: _____

Address: _____

_____ Zip: _____